— THE BIG BOOK OF THE —

CIVIL WAR

Fascinating Facts about the Civil War, Including Historic Photographs, Maps, and Documents

by Joanne Mattern

COURAGE
BOOKS

AN IMPRINT OF RUNNING PRESS
PHILADELPHIA • LONDON

9 8 7 6 5 4 3 2 1
Digit on the right indicates the number of this printing

Library of Congress Control Number: 2006932680

ISBN-10: 0-7624-2856-2
ISBN-13: 978-0-7624-2856-4

Cover and interior design by Alicia Freile
Edited by T. L. Bonaddio and Gregory J. W. Urwin
Photo research by Susan Oyama
Typography: Adobe Garamond, ITC Officina Sans, and Caslon Antique VL.

This book may be ordered by mail from the publisher.
But try your bookstore first!

Published by Courage Books, an imprint of
Running Press Book Publishers
2300 Chestnut Street, Suite 200
Philadelphia, PA 19103-4371

Visit us on the web!
www.runningpress.com

Picture Credits

Cover art and photographs clockwise from top left:

Arsenal grounds, Richmond, VA. Library of Congress, LC-DIG-cwpb-02740

The USS Monitor fighting the CSS Merrimack [Virginia] at the Battle of Hampton Broads during the American Civil War, 9th March 1862. Private Collection, Peter Newark American Pictures/The Bridgeman Art Library International

Capture of Fort Fisher. Library of Congress, LC-USZC4-1731

Abraham Lincoln. Hulton Archive/Getty Images

Clara Barton, c.1865. Schlesinger Library, Radcliffe Institute, Harvard University/The Bridgeman Art Library International

Come and Join Us Brothers, Union recruiting poster aimed at black volunteers. Private Collection, Peter Newark American Pictures/The Bridgeman Art Library International

Col. William W. Averell and staff, 3d Pennsylvania Cavalry, Westover Landing,Va. Library of Congress, LC-DIG-cwpb-04061

Sheridan's Ride. Library of Congress, LC-USZC4-1964

Jefferson Davis. Library of Congress, LC-DIG-cwpbh-00879

Table of Contents

Introduction: The United States in the Mid-1800s

Life in the United States was very different in the mid-1800s than it is today. At that time, much of the country was rural. Vast distances separated most towns and villages. While there were several large cities, such as Boston, New York, Baltimore, Chicago, Philadelphia, and New Orleans, most of the population lived far away from crowded urban areas. At this time in United States history, agriculture was the main occupation. Most people lived on farms or in rural villages.

By the mid-1800s, the U.S. faced the important and divisive issue of slavery.

Textile mills helped drive the industrialization of the Northeast.

In the 1850s, the United States was still a young country. The nation had only won its independence from Great Britain in 1783, less than one hundred years earlier. In the years since then, the United States had found its strength as a nation. By 1860, the United States was the fourth largest manufacturing power in the world. The nation was now large enough and rich enough that

European nations were beginning to take notice and give the United States a new respect.

At home, the country was growing at an astonishing rate. Settlers pushed into parts of the country that had previously been the home of Native Americans. As these settlers pushed Native Americans out of their homelands, they brought their way of life and founded their own societies in the vast spaces of the Midwest and the Far West.

The middle years of the 1800s were also a time of great change. The Industrial Revolution had come to the United States. While the nation's economy was still mainly agricultural, factories were becoming more important. This was especially true in the Northern part of the nation. Textile mills and other factories used steam power and other machines to do work that once could only be done by hand. This wave of industrialization would change the country forever.

1790
The first American cotton mill begins operating in Pawtucket, Rhode Island.

Rhode Island

1793
Fugitive Slave Act is passed.

1793
Eli Whitney invents the cotton gin.

4

Plantations grew crops such as cotton and were worked almost entirely by slaves.

During the mid-1800s, the United States faced many challenges. Although the nation had always been divided along geographical lines, these differences became more intense during the mid-1800s. The Northern states—those in New England, New York, New Jersey, and Pennsylvania—became more industrialized. Immigrants from Europe moved into Northern cities, providing cheap labor for the factories springing up all over the landscape. The territories of the Midwest were becoming states as well, opening the frontier to hard-working settlers who headed west for a new life and the freedom to claim cheap land for farms. Canals and railroads soon linked the Northeast and Northwest into one economic unit commonly known as the North. Meanwhile, the Southern states—Virginia, North and South Carolina, Texas, Kentucky, Maryland, Missouri, Delaware, Tennessee, Arkansas, Louisiana, Mississippi, Alabama, Georgia, and Florida—remained tied to an agricultural economy based on plantations. Plantations were large estates that grew crops such as cotton, sugar cane, rice, and tobacco. These plantations needed twenty or more workers to function. Those workers were almost entirely black slaves from Africa.

By 1850, slavery had become the most important and divisive issue the United States had ever faced. Most people in the North and the West felt slavery was morally wrong and economically unnecessary. Most Southerners saw slavery as a necessary and traditional part of Southern life and business. Slaves were the personal property of their owners, these people argued, and the U.S. Constitution protected personal property, didn't it? The Constitution also acknowledged slavery through the 3/5 Compromise, which stated that a slave was worth 3/5 of a white man when counting residents for congressional representation.

Before the 1850s, decades of compromise between the Northern and the Southern states kept the country together. But as the 1850s drew to a close, those compromises began breaking apart with the passage of the Fugitive Slave Act of 1850 and the Kansas-Nebraska Act of 1854. Nothing could stop the nation's terrible slide into civil war.

1808
Congress passes a law prohibiting the importation of any new slaves.

1820
The Missouri Compromise prohibits slavery anywhere north of Missouri's southern border.

1831
Nat Turner leads a slave rebellion in Virginia.

How the War Began

The problems that would tear the United States apart in the Civil War had been brewing for a long time. The two key issues were slavery and states' rights.

Slavery had been introduced into the United States during Colonial times. However, it was outlawed in the Northern part of the country following the American Revolution. Most people in the Northern states considered slavery to be unacceptable and even evil.

Many people in the Southern states had a very different opinion of slavery. The Southern economy depended on slavery. Slaves were needed to pick cotton, sugar, rice, and other crops and run the huge plantations that made up the South's agricultural economy. Most Southerners had grown up with slavery and felt it was a natural, normal part of life. They viewed slaves not as people, but as property. Many White Southerners also claimed that slavery was sanctioned by the Bible. In addition, they not only considered slaves property, but also as savages who had to be kept under control lest they rise up and destroy the master race.

When the United States government agreed with the North and tried to set limits on slavery, a new problem emerged. Southern states wanted slavery to be legal. Did each state have the right to make its own laws? Or did states have to follow federal laws, even if they didn't agree with them? Although several court cases declared the federal government had supreme authority over all of the United States, not all Southerners were happy with this—especially when it came to slavery.

During the middle of the 1800s, many new states were being added to the Union (another name for the United States). Every time a state was added, politicians debated whether it should allow slavery or not. These politicians tried very hard to keep the number of slave states the same as the number of free states, so that one side would not overpower the other. This was not always an easy task!

Back in 1820, the Missouri Compromise had admitted Maine as a free state, while Missouri was admitted as a slave state. This kept the country in balance by keeping the numbers of free and slave states the same. The Compromise also said that no state north of Missouri's southern border would be a slave state. However,

In the 1850s, most Northerners, including American abolitionist Wendell Phillips, considered slavery to be unacceptable.

1839

Slaves on board the ship *Amistad* take control of the ship near Cuba and sail to Connecticut. They are captured, but the Supreme Court later releases the slaves and says they are free.

Conflict had raged between pro-slavery raiders and anti-slavery militias in Kansas.

everything changed in 1854 when Congress passed the Kansas-Nebraska Act. The act was introduced by Senator Stephen A. Douglas. Douglas said that the residents of Kansas and Nebraska were the only ones who should decide whether to allow slavery or not, not the federal government.

Northerners were outraged. The Kansas-Nebraska Act erased the boundaries set up by the Missouri Compromise and allowed slavery to spread into Northern territory. Private anti-slavery organizations in the Northern states raised money to send settlers into the area, while other Northerners went to Kansas for cheap land and opportunity. They opposed the introduction of blacks into the territory because they did not want to compete with cheap black labor. In addition, they just did not want any black neighbors—free or slave. At the same time, Southern newspapers urged white Southerners to move to Kansas. Soon pro-slavery Missourians, who did not want a free state on their western border, swept into Kansas at election time to terrorize free state voters into staying away from the polls and to submit multiple ballots for pro-slavery candidates. Violence soon flared up between the two

groups. Pro-slavery raiders fought anti-slavery militias throughout the territories with cannons, guns, and swords.

In 1856, the violence spread to the federal government itself. Charles Sumner, a senator from Massachusetts, stood on the floor of the Senate for two days speaking against slavery. He criticized South Carolina Senator Andrew Pickens Butler. A few days later, Butler's nephew, South Carolina Congressman Preston Brooks, burst into the Senate to avenge his uncle. He attacked Sumner, beating him with a cane, and it took three years for the older man to fully recover from his injuries. The incident further divided the nation. South Carolina residents applauded Brooks as a hero defending his family honor, while Northern residents were horrified at the violence. Things would only get worse.

1850
The Compromise of 1850 is proposed by Henry Clay. The Compromise divided territory gained from Mexico and spelled out which territories would allow slavery. The Compromise also included a harsher new Fugitive Slave Law.

1852
Harriet Beecher Stowe publishes *Uncle Tom's Cabin,* a novel that dramatized the cruelty of slavery.

135,000 SETS, 270,000 VOLUMES SOLD.

UNCLE TOM'S CABIN

FOR SALE HERE.

AN EDITION FOR THE MILLION, COMPLETE IN 1 Vol., PRICE 37 1-2 CENTS.
"   IN GERMAN, IN 1 Vol., PRICE 50 CENTS.
"   IN 2 Vols., CLOTH, 6 PLATES, PRICE $1.50.
SUPERB ILLUSTRATED EDITION, IN 1 Vol., WITH 153 ENGRAVINGS,
PRICES FROM $2.50 TO $5.00.

The Greatest Book of the Age.

Northern Life

While most Northerners still lived and worked on farms, this part of the United States was becoming more and more industrialized. Factories, mills, and other businesses were built at a fast pace. These businesses used water and steam to run machinery. This machinery, in turn, made products. Before the Industrial Revolution, for example, every piece of clothing had to be made by hand, one piece at a time. After the Industrial Revolution, a cotton mill could produce cotton thread and cotton cloth. Meanwhile, the invention of the sewing machine by Elias Howe in the 1840s greatly accelerated the manufacture of clothing and later shoes.

While machines cut down on the number of workers needed to complete a task, people were still needed to run the machines. The North found many new sources of cheap labor. Families from depressed rural areas were the first factory workers. Many farmers' wives who had been sewing clothes at home found jobs in factories. So did unskilled agricultural workers who wanted a steadier source of income than seasonal employment.

Although the work was tedious and often dangerous, a job in a cotton mill was one of the few opportunities available to young, unmarried teenage girls. For these girls, a job in a mill gave them a small bit of financial independence, a way to live in the exciting "big city," and their first taste of freedom and life away from home.

Girls and young women, like the "Lowell Mill Girls" in Massachusetts, worked in cotton mills.

Soon children joined the work force. Boys and girls as young as four years old were recruited to work in factories and mills. For these children, earning a few pennies a day was a valuable way to contribute to the family income and was considered much more important than going to school.

Immigrants were a third group that provided cheap labor for Northern industries. Just to find a job in America, these workers accepted less money, and they took on the jobs few others wanted. During the 1840s, a potato famine devastated Ireland and forced many families to emigrate to America or starve. The Irish were joined by other immigrants, particularly from Germany and the Scandinavian countries, who were escaping from war or seeking religious freedom in America. Although many immigrants settled in New Orleans and other areas of the South, most immigrants

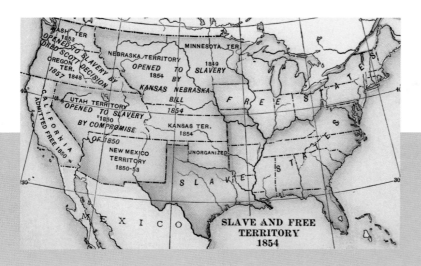

1854
The Kansas-Nebraska Act is passed.

1856
Southerner Preston Brooks attacks Northern Senator Charles Sumner in the Senate.

Charles Sumner

Some American settlers traveled west instead of staying in Northern cities.

Industrial Power

Numbers tell the story of the North's industrial power. In 1860, when the Civil War was about to start, there were 23 states in the Union (the part of the nation that remained loyal to the federal government). The population of these states was 22 million. The North also had 110,000 factories which employed more than a million workers. There were more than 20,000 miles of railroad track in the Northern states, as well as 96 percent of the nation's railroad equipment. These railroads became increasingly important as industry grew, because they provided a quick and reliable way to ship goods from one part of the country to another. Later, when the Civil War began, they would be used to ship armies and war supplies as well.

The North had 110,000 factories, including the Boott Cotton Mills in Lowell, Massachusetts.

settled in Northern cities. Others traveled west to build farming communities in Pennsylvania, and the Midwest.

Farm life was still important in the North, but machines changed farming, too. Chores that were once done by hand or by using animals began to be done more quickly and easily by machines. Also, most farms in the North were fairly small. Because the North never had the vast plantations that the South depended on, it did not have the need for a large amount of cheap labor to produce agricultural goods. Things were very different in the South, where plantation agriculture rested on cash crops that were labor intensive and had long growing seasons. These factors meant that Southern planters needed a large workforce that was available year round and could be easily controlled. Slavery, as inhumane as it was, met that need.

1857
The Supreme Court decides that Dred Scott is a slave. Scott had sued for his freedom, claiming he was entitled to freedom because he and his master had lived in the free territory of Minnesota for two years.

1858
Abraham Lincoln and Stephen Douglas run for the U.S. Senate in Illinois. Their debates bring Lincoln to national attention, but he loses the race to Douglas.

Southern Life

While life in the North grew more industrial, life in the South continued much as it had since the first settlers arrived two hundred years earlier. The hot, wet climate of the South was ideal for growing a large number of crops that attracted high prices in the world market. At first, tobacco was the main Southern crop, but by the late 1700s, that crop had ruined the soil and was no longer profitable. At the same time, textile mills in the northern United States and Great Britain were demanding cotton to weave into cloth. Unfortunately, Southern farmers could not remove the seeds from enough cotton to fill that demand.

There were two kinds of cotton. Black seed cotton was grown in the West Indies and Brazil, as well as the Sea Islands along the Georgia and South Carolina coast. This type of cotton was easy to clean, but it would not grow in the drier Southern soil. The other kind of cotton was green seed cotton, and it grew like a weed in the South. The problem with green seed cotton was removing the pesky seeds in order to make the cotton fit for weaving. The seeds were so sticky that it was almost impossible to pull them from the soft cotton fibers. Slaves did this job, but one slave could clean only a pound of cotton a day. This meant that frustrated Southern planters had the land to plant plenty of cotton, but they could not produce enough clean cotton to send to the mills to make it a profitable export.

Eli Whitney's cotton gin revolutionized Southern farming.

John Brown

1859
Abolitionist John Brown attacks the federal government's arsenal at Harpers Ferry, hoping to steal enough guns to start an armed slave rebellion. He is captured and later executed.

November 6, 1860
Abraham Lincoln is elected president of the United States.

Prior to the invention of the cotton gin, one slave could clean only one pound of cotton a day.

The South vs. The North

When the Civil War started, there were eleven Southern states in the Confederacy. About nine million people lived in these states, and about 3.5 million of them were slaves. There were only 20,000 factories in the Confederate states, with only 110,000 employees. The South had only 9,000 miles of railroad track, less than half of what the North had.

Perhaps because of its smaller size, the South had always felt somewhat bullied by the North. Its people felt that Northerners were deliberately trying to provoke a racial war by agitating the slavery question. Southerners cherished their way of life and resented anyone who said it was morally wrong or who wanted to change it. As the years passed and the threat of ending slavery grew stronger, Southerners became more determined to use whatever means necessary to hold onto slavery and their very lives.

What the plantation owners needed was a machine to remove the seeds. In 1793, Eli Whitney invented just such a machine. He called it the cotton gin, and it revolutionized Southern farming. The cotton gin allowed one worker to remove the seeds from as much as eighty pounds of cotton a day.

Eli Whitney's cotton gin changed agriculture in the Southern United States forever. The South now had a crop it could grow easily and sell for a great profit. Ship builders had a valuable cargo to deliver to Northern and British ports, and Northern factories had a product they desperately needed. The importance of cotton also revived the plantation system and the vast number of slaves needed to run it. This social development would eventually lead to the U.S. Civil War.

Cotton was one of the South's main crops.

December 20, 1860
South Carolina becomes the first state to secede from the Union.

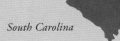

South Carolina

January 1861
Florida, Alabama, Georgia, Mississippi, Texas, and Louisiana secede from the Union.

February 9, 1861
The Confederate States of America is formed and Jefferson Davis is elected president.

Jefferson Davis

Slavery

When the first settlers came to the United States from Europe during the early 1600s, they brought white indentured servants with them. Indentured servants had signed a contract agreeing to work for someone for a specific number of years. In return, the employer agreed to pay for the servant's passage to America, and also to provide food, clothes, and a place for him or her to live. After the servant had worked for the required number of years, he or she was free.

In the early days of the American colonies, the system of indentured servants worked. However, Bacon's Rebellion, an uprising by indentured servants which rocked Virginia in 1676, showed the planter class how dangerous the indentured servant system could be. Indentured servants were mostly young Englishmen with guns. Even though they were servants, the fact that they were English meant they had the right to carry weapons. Slaves could be kept disarmed, and had no rights in the eyes of the law. In addition, they did not have to be freed when their term of service ended. Also, slaves' children became the property of their masters, which further enlarged the workforce. At the same time, America needed more cheap labor to work its farms. Slavery provided the answer. By the late 1600s, slaves were common throughout the Northern and Southern colonies. After the United States won its independence at the end of the American Revolution in 1783, slavery continued in some parts of the new nation.

However, the American Revolution, which claimed that "all men are created equal," forced many Americans to question slavery. By 1804, many Northern states had passed laws to end slavery.

The Triangular Trade

Slaves were almost always imported from Africa as part of a route called the Triangular Trade. Ships left New England with rum, guns, iron, cotton, grain, and other goods. These ships sailed to Africa, where their cargo was exchanged for slaves that had been captured by local agents. The ships then sailed to the West Indies, where some slaves were traded for sugar and molasses. Finally, the ships returned to New England and other American ports with slaves and their cargo, which was used to make rum and start the cycle all over again.

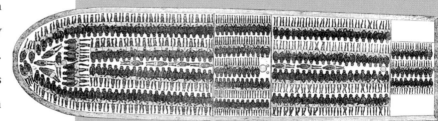

The interior of a slave ship

Some Southern states wanted to do the same thing but could not because it would destroy their economy. The North was more industrial and used more machines to produce its crops and other products. These machines could do the work of several people, which cut down on the amount of cheap labor that was needed. Things were very different in the South, however. The South had an agricultural economy that relied almost entirely on people pick-

February 23, 1861
Texas secedes from the Union.

March 4, 1861
Abraham Lincoln is sworn in as the nation's 16th president.

April 12, 1861
Confederate troops attack Fort Sumter, beginning the Civil War.

Slaves were originally transported from Africa on ships like the Wildfire.

ing crops. Southern plantation owners could not do the work themselves and they could not afford to pay large numbers of workers. The answer was cheap labor: slaves.

Between ten and twelve million Africans were taken to the Americas as slaves. Most ended up working in Caribbean sugar fields, but between 600,000 and 700,000 were sent to the American colonies. By 1860, there were almost four million slaves in the United States.

A slave's life was extremely difficult. Slaves were sold at slave auctions. Here, men and women were lined up for potential buyers to see them. Slaves were described like animals, and slave owners were only interested in those who were strong enough to work.

TO BE SOLD,
A Likely negro Man, his Wife and Child ; the negro Man capable of doing all forts of Plantation Work, and a good Miller : The Woman exceeding fit for a Farmer, being capable of doing any Work, belonging to a Houfe in the Country, at reasonable Rates, inquire of the Printer hereof.

Slaves could be sold by their masters at any time.

Other slaves were born into this life. Any baby born to a slave woman was automatically the property of the woman's owner.

No matter where a slave worked, his or her life was filled with hardships. Most slaves lived in unheated shacks with dirt floors. They received a poor diet. Depending on their master, disobedient slaves could be whipped, chained, or suffer other brutal punishments. Slaves could be sold at any time, and families were often split up when one or more members were sold to another owner. A slave had no say about anything in his or her life. Slaves were the property of their master and had to do whatever the master demanded.

Slaves who tried to escape were hunted down like criminals. Many people earned money by capturing fugitive, or runaway, slaves to collect a reward from the slave's master. The Fugitive Slave Act of 1850 said that any Northern man could be forced to assist in the recovery of runaway slaves, whether he wanted to or not. Other slaves were killed as they tried to avoid capture. It was a harsh life that offered very little promise. Religion was the greatest source of hope for slaves, as well as a source of hope that they would eventually reach the Promised Land—freedom.

Field and House Slaves

Slaves could be divided into two types: field slaves and house slaves. Field slaves performed the back-breaking labor of picking crops in the hot sun, as well as other farm work, such as handling animals. House slaves had it slightly easier. These slaves worked inside the plantation household. They cooked, cleaned, took care of the owner's children, and performed other household chores. Other slaves were hired out to masters in Southern cities.

April 15, 1861
President Lincoln calls for 75,000 army volunteers.

April 17, 1861
Virginia secedes from the Union.

April 19, 1861
President Lincoln orders a naval blockade of all Confederate ports.

Virginia

Free the Slaves!

Some Northerners were horrified by slavery. Members of a religious group called the Quakers believed slavery was morally wrong. So did other Northerners. People who worked to end slavery through moral or political action were called abolitionists, because they wanted to abolish, or end, slavery. Abolitionists worked in different ways to try to end slavery. Some published newspapers or pamphlets describing the evils of slavery. One of the most famous was William Lloyd Garrison, who published an abolitionist newspaper called *The Liberator.* Garrison demanded immediate emancipation without compensation to slaveholders. He wrote, "On this subject, I do not wish to think, or speak, or write with moderation. No! No! Tell a man whose house is on fire, to give a moderate alarm . . . tell the mother to gradually extricate her babe from the fire into which it has fallen; —but urge me not to use moderation in a cause like the present. I am in earnest—I will not equivocate—I will not excuse—I will not retreat a single inch—AND I WILL BE HEARD." Others formed organizations such as the American Anti-Slavery Society and the American Colonization Society, which encouraged sending freed slaves back to Africa.

Some abolitionists and slaves took a violent approach. In August 1831, a slave named Nat Turner led a rebellion in Virginia that killed 57 whites along with most of the slaves that took part. His revolt made the white South see Garrison and the abolitionist movement as a bigger threat than they actually were. Southerners blamed the rebellion on abolitionist teachers instead of acknowledging that slaves wanted freedom. In 1859, another abolitionist, John Brown, attacked the federal government arsenal at Harpers Ferry, Virginia. Brown hoped to steal enough guns to arm slaves and start a rebellion. Both Turner and Brown were arrested and executed.

Abolitionists included many former slaves. These runaways became well-known for their writings and speeches against slavery. One of the most famous was Sojourner Truth, who escaped from her master in New York in 1827 and began lecturing on abolition in 1843. Her book, *The Narrative of Sojourner Truth,* became a bestseller before the Civil War. Another was Frederick Douglass,

Sojourner Truth, one of the most famous abolitionists

William Lloyd Garrison published an abolitionist newspaper called The Liberator.

May 1861
Richmond, Virginia, becomes the capital of the Confederacy.

May 6, 1861
Arkansas and Tennessee secede from the Union.

May 20, 1861
North Carolina secedes from the Union.

North Carolina

Frederick Douglass

who escaped from slavery, received an education in the North, and became a well-known speaker and author. His publications include the newspaper, *The North Star*, as well as his best-selling autobiography, *Narrative of the Life of Frederick Douglass, an American Slave.*

Beginning in the 1820s, some Northerners became part of the Underground Railroad. The Underground Railroad was not an actual railroad, but a system of secret trails that led from Southern slave states to freedom in the North. Guides, called "conductors," led escaped slaves through the South, often hiding in the woods or at the homes of friendly white settlers. These homes were called "stations." Once the slaves reached the free states of the North, they could settle down and start a new life, or continue on the Underground Railroad to Canada, where slavery was illegal. One of the most famous Underground Railroad conductors was Harriet Tubman, who was an escaped slave herself.

Harriet Tubman, famous Underground Railroad conductor

The U.S. Census lists only 6,000 slaves escaping on the Underground Railroad from 1818 to 1850, but there were probably many more. Some historians believe between 30,000 and 100,000 people escaped slavery on the Underground Railroad during those years. At least 30,000 slaves escaped to Canada, with 1,000 settling in the Toronto area alone.

Fugitive Slave Law

Southern anger led to the passage of the Fugitive Slave Law in 1850. This law said that fugitive slaves had to be returned to their owners, even if they had already lived in freedom in the North. It also punished anyone who helped a fugitive slave with a $1,000 fine and six months in jail, as well as anyone who refused to catch slaves. Even white Northerners who did not like blacks did not want to be forced to catch runaways. They felt white Southerners were using federal power to make slaves out of their Northern cousins. The Fugitive Slave Law only increased the tensions between North and South. Frederick Douglass summed up the anger of many Northerners when he said, "The only way to make the Fugitive Slave Law a dead letter is to make half a dozen or more dead kidnappers."

However, the fact that Northerners were actively helping escaped slaves made Southerners very angry. They felt that their very way of life was being threatened by outsiders, and that they had to protect their way of life at any cost. South Carolina Senator John C. Calhoun summed up this feeling when he said, "Let us show at least as much spirit in defending our rights as the Abolitionists have . . . in denouncing them." Another Southern politician, Congressman Henry A. Wise of Virginia, said "They [Northerners] cannot attack the institutions of slavery without attacking the institutions of the country, our safety, and welfare."

The First Battle of Bull Run

Summer 1861
The U.S. Sanitary Commission is formed to aid injured soldiers.

July 21, 1861
The First Battle of Bull Run is fought, ending with a surprising victory for the Confederacy.

The Election of 1860

As the presidential election of 1860 approached, slavery became a central issue in almost every candidate's campaign.

In April 1860, the Democratic Party held its convention to nominate a candidate for president. During the convention, 48 delegates from eight Southern states walked out because the party refused to guarantee the constitutional rights of slave owners. In June, another convention was held, and this time 110 Southern delegates walked out. The men who were left wanted a candidate who would work toward a compromise between North and South. They chose Senator Stephen A. Douglas. Douglas was from Illinois and was very popular and well-known.

The Southern Democrats who had walked out of the convention met to choose their own candidate. They chose John C. Breckinridge, who was then serving as Vice President under President James Buchanan. Breckinridge was from Kentucky, which was a slave state. He called for the federal government to "protect the rights of persons and property in the Territories and wherever else its Constitutional authority extended."

Meanwhile, the Republican Party had already had its convention and chosen its candidate. The Republican Party had sprung to life after the passage of the Kansas-Nebraska Act to oppose the spread of slavery into the federal territories. Republicans believed if they could stop the growth of slavery, it would gradually die. Their choice was Abraham Lincoln. Lincoln

On November 6, 1860, Abraham Lincoln won the presidential election.

was a lawyer from Illinois who had little experience in the government. He was chosen because his views on slavery were more moderate than other possible candidates. However, pro-slavery

July 22, 1861
A Congressional resolution states that the war is to preserve the Union, not end slavery.

July 27, 1861
Lincoln names General George B. McClellan as the head of the Army of the Potomac, the largest force of the Union Army.

August 10, 1861
Confederates win Battle of Wilson's Creek, the first major battle fought west of the Mississippi River.

Southern Democrats chose John C. Breckinridge as their presidential candidate.

In June 1860, Stephen A. Douglas was nominated by Northern Democrats and closely raced Lincoln to the presidency.

Southerners despised Lincoln and vowed to secede, or leave the Union, if he won the election. Lincoln's name was not even on the ballot in Southern states. Even Southerners who did not own slaves felt that electing Lincoln would give the North too much power and bring an end to the Southern way of life.

In those days, candidates did not campaign publicly, as they do today. Instead, their supporters did most of the work. Each candidate's supporters traveled around the nation, making speeches and passing around photographs of the man they wanted to win. Parades and rallies also spread the word.

Finally, the votes were cast. Breckinridge carried all but four slave states and received 849,000 votes—not enough to win the election. The race came down to Douglas and Lincoln. Douglas received 1,375,000 votes. Lincoln received 1,866,000 votes, mostly in Northern and Western states with large populations. Even though he had won, Lincoln had little popular support in most of the country. It was clear that his election was only the start of more trouble for the United States.

November 1, 1861
Lincoln names McClellan as General-in-Chief of the Union Army.

January 11, 1862
Edwin M. Stanton becomes Lincoln's second Secretary of War.

February 1862
Julia Ward Howe's poem, "The Battle Hymn of the Republic," first appears in a magazine called *The Atlantic Monthly*. The poem will later become the unofficial anthem of the Union.

Secession!

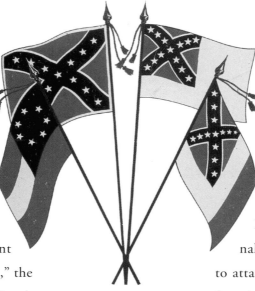

Confederate States of America flags from 1861 to 1865

It did not take long for the South to act after Lincoln won the presidential election on November 6, 1860. Just six weeks later, on December 20, a secession convention was held in Charleston, South Carolina. Delegates voted that the state should secede from the Union. In a document called "Declaration of the Causes of Secession," the delegates stated, "We, therefore, the people of South Carolina, by our delegates in the Convention assembled . . . have solemnly declared that the Union heretofore existing between this State and the other States of North America is dissolved."

South Carolina began to prepare for war. On December 27, its militia seized Fort Moultrie and took over the federal arsenal in Charleston. The militia also made plans to attack Fort Sumter, one of the most important forts in the area. In the first few months of 1861, South Carolina troops surrounded the fort and prevented supplies from getting through.

The cabinet of the Confederate States of America, 1861

February 16, 1862
General Ulysses S. Grant captures a Confederate army at Fort Donelson, Tennessee, the first major Union victory of the war.

February 25, 1862
Union troops capture Nashville, Tennessee, without a fight.

March 7-8, 1862
Union victory at Pea Ridge, Arkansas, dooms Confederate hopes of conquering Missouri.

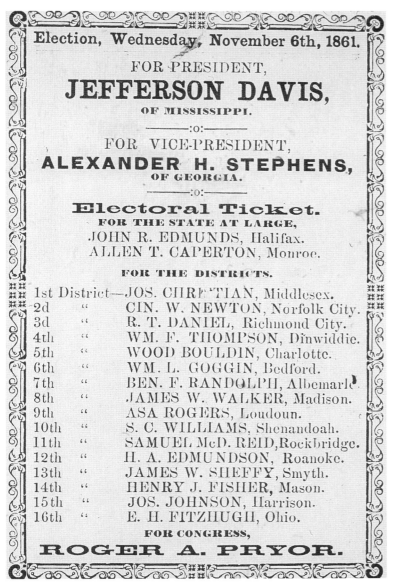

Jefferson Davis became president of the Confederate States of America in February, 1861.

Meanwhile, other states were following South Carolina's lead and seceding from the Union. By the end of February 1861, Florida, Alabama, Georgia, Mississippi, Louisiana, and Texas had also seceded.

In February, 1861, delegates from the first six states that had seceded met to form a new government. They called their country the Confederate States of America and elected Jefferson Davis as their president on February 9. After Lincoln's inauguration on March 4, 1861, Davis sent his vice president, Alexander Hamilton

Stephens, and several delegates to meet with the new president. Lincoln refused to see them.

Now all attention turned to Fort Sumter in Charleston, South Carolina's harbor. At the time, there were 119 men in the fort, including 76 soldiers and 43 civilian workers. The fort was in serious trouble. There was little food or water inside because South Carolina's cannons kept Northern ships away from the fort, and local grocers refused to sell food to a federal fort. Still, Anderson was determined to hold the fort.

Anderson faced a militia under the command of General Pierre G. T. Beauregard. Beauregard demanded that Anderson surrender the fort. Anderson refused, telling Beauregard, "I will await the first shot." That shot came at 4:30 in the morning of April 12, when Beauregard's cannons fired on the fort. Within hours, forty-three guns around the fort had fired more than four thousand shells.

By the next day, Fort Sumter was on fire. Although Anderson fired 1,000 rounds of ammunition, he knew that without enough supplies or soldiers, he was beaten. On April 13, he surrendered the fort to Beauregard. The Civil War had begun.

The Civil War began with the attack on Fort Sumter in Charleston harbor, South Carolina.

March 9, 1862
The USS Monitor and the CSS Virginia face off in the first confrontation between two ironclad ships. The battle is a draw.

March 11, 1862
Lincoln demotes McClellan to command only the Army of the Potomac and announces that all Union commanders now report directly to the Secretary of War.

April 6–7, 1862
The Battle of Shiloh ends with a Union victory for General Ulysses S. Grant

Abraham Lincoln and Jefferson Davis

ABRAHAM LINCOLN

(1809–1865)

Abraham Lincoln grew up to become the sixteenth president of the United States. However, this man of great power had very humble beginnings. Lincoln was born on February 12, 1809, in a simple log cabin in Kentucky. His mother died when Lincoln was a child, and his father remarried soon afterward. Lincoln and his family were poor and worked very hard to survive. There was little time for school. However, Lincoln loved to read and to learn. He borrowed books from neighbors and taught himself to read, write, do math, and other basic skills. Lincoln liked to read so much that he often held a book in one hand while he pushed a plow or did other farm chores with the other! He knew that reading was the key to a better life.

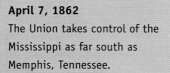

Abraham Lincoln, the 16th President of the United States of America

Despite Lincoln's very tall and awkward physical appearance, he got along with people and was well-liked by almost everyone he knew. People especially admired his honesty and his gift for public speaking. Lincoln opened a small law office in Springfield, Illinois, and became active in local politics. In 1846, Lincoln was elected to Congress. However, he did not seek re-election when his term expired in 1848. Instead, he returned home to Springfield.

Lincoln was very upset by the Kansas-Nebraska Act, and his fears brought him back into national politics. Lincoln was afraid that slavery was going to spread throughout the United States and tear the country apart. In 1856, he joined the Republican Party, which had been formed only a few years before. In 1858, Lincoln ran for the Senate against Stephen Douglas, but lost after a series of public debates. However, those debates brought Lincoln to national attention and gave him a great deal of support when the Republicans were looking for a presidential candidate in 1860. Lincoln won the election and became the first Republican president of the United States.

Although Lincoln did not like slavery and felt that it must end, his real goal was the survival of the United States. He felt that the United States was the freest nation in the world because of its democratic foundations and he was determined to do everything in his power to keep the Union together.

April 7, 1862
The Union takes control of the Mississippi as far south as Memphis, Tennessee.

April 16, 1862
Confederate President Jefferson Davis signs the Conscription Act. It is the first draft in American history.

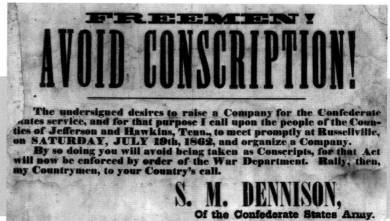

JEFFERSON DAVIS

(1808–1889)

Jefferson Davis was the Confederate States of America's one and only president. It was a position he never asked for and did not really want. Davis was born in a log cabin in Kentucky on June 3, 1808. Soon afterward, his family moved to Mississippi, where they became cotton farmers.

Davis grew into a confident, intelligent, wealthy young man. He first attended college but later transferred to West Point, the nation's training school for army officers, where he graduated in 1828. After graduation, he served in the army in Wisconsin, Illinois, and Indian Territory, which is now the state of Oklahoma. In 1835, he left the army and retired to a

Jefferson Davis, President of the Confederate States of America

plantation in Mississippi, which he owned with his brother. Davis was considered to be unusually gentle in his treatment of his slaves. Whippings were forbidden, and slaves were allowed to grow their own food and keep the money they earned by selling eggs laid by their own chickens.

In 1844, Davis was elected to the U.S. House of Representatives. He served until 1846, when he resigned to fight in the Mexican-American War. Davis became a war hero. In 1847, the governor of Mississippi appointed him to fill an empty Senate seat. Davis served until 1850. Later, he served as Secretary of War under President Franklin Pierce, and had another term in the Senate from 1857 until 1861, when the Civil War began. On January 21, 1861, Davis announced the secession of Mississippi and resigned from the Senate. Less than a month later, he was chosen as the first president of the Confederacy.

In 1858, Abraham Lincoln and Stephen A. Douglas held a series of public debates.

April 25, 1862
New Orleans, the largest city in the Confederacy, falls to Union naval forces under Captain David G. Farragut.

May 14, 1862
General McClellan comes within six miles of Richmond, Virginia, but fails to continue into the Confederate capital.

May 20, 1862
Lincoln signs the Homestead Act, which guarantees 160 acres of land to anyone who lives on it for five years and improves it, and encourages the settlement of the West.

June 6, 1862
Memphis, Tennessee, falls to Union forces.

Commanders of the North and South

Many in the North thought the war would be over quickly, with a Northern victory. However, the South won many of the early battles, especially in Virginia. Both the Union and the Confederacy were shocked by the great loss of life. One out of every three Confederate soldiers died, as did one out of five Union soldiers.

Many people felt that the commanders of the Union Army were to blame for the North's failure to win the war quickly. Because of these doubts, Lincoln appointed several different commanders in the early years of the war. At first, General Winfield Scott was the leader of the Union Army. Scott had been a commander in the Mexican-American War, but he did not impress anyone in the Civil War. In November, 1861, Lincoln replaced Scott with General George B. McClellan, who had already served as the commander of the Army of the Potomac, the North's largest field army, based on Washington, D.C. McClellan lost his position as the Union Army's commanding general in early 1862

Under McClellan's command, the North claimed the Battle of Antietam a victory.

General George B. McClellan
(1826–1885)

McClellan was born in 1826 and served in the military until he resigned in 1857. After he left the army, he became vice president of the Illinois Central Railroad. When the Civil War started, thirty-five-year-old McClellan rejoined the army and was given the rank of major general. He organized

At thirty-five, George B. McClellan rejoined the army at the start of the Civil War and was ranked as major general.

and led the Army of the Potomac. Although McClellan's troops liked and respected him, many others saw him as a coward who was unwilling to take chances. Lincoln blamed McClellan for the South's unexpected victories in many battles.

July 1862
Congress allows blacks to join the military.

July 11, 1862
Lincoln names Henry W. Halleck General-in-Chief.

August 29–30, 1862
The Second Battle of Bull Run is fought, again ending in a Southern victory.

Ulysses S. Grant
(1822–1885)

Like McClellan, Grant was an army officer who had resigned and then returned to the military at the start of the war. Grant was a tough commander, and Lincoln greatly admired him. His first major victory was at Fort Donelson, Tennessee, in February, 1862. Grant's heavy attacks

General Grant led the North to win the Civil War.

against Confederate forces won the Battle of Vicksburg in 1863. In March 1864, Lincoln gave Grant command over all the Union armies. The tide of the war had turned. Just over a year later, Grant forced Confederate general Robert E. Lee to surrender. The North had won. Grant rode his popularity into the White House, serving as president from 1869 to 1877. After he left office, Grant wrote his memoirs. The book was a huge success and is still considered to be one of the best accounts of the Civil War.

so he could focus all his attention on commanding the Army of the Potomac. In July 1862, General Henry Wager Halleck was named general-in-chief of all the Union armies, while Ambrose Burnside took command of the Army of the Potamac.

Following several other changes in command, Lincoln finally found his supreme commander in Ulysses S. Grant, who succeeded Halleck as general-in-chief in March 1864.

Unlike the North, the South relied mostly on many generals to run its army. Its best general was Robert E. Lee from Virginia. Lee assumed command of the Army of Northern Virginia in the spring of 1862, and held that job to the war's end. He was also

named general-in-chief of the Confederate armies on February 6, 1865. He held that post until his surrender two months later.

Lee was a brilliant general. He used clever strategies to defeat the much larger Union armies in battle after battle. However, Lee lost many of his generals and soldiers in battle and that, combined with the Union's larger numbers, stronger industry, and larger financial resources, eventually drove Lee and the Confederacy into defeat. Even at his best, Lee could be overly aggressive and attacked too much. In even his greatest victories, he lost a higher percentage of his troops than the enemy, which the badly outnumbered Confederacy could not afford. After the war, Lee became president of Washington College in Virginia. Today, the school is called Washington and Lee University in his honor. Lee remains one of the South's greatest heroes and is still admired today.

Robert E. Lee
(1807–1870)

Lee was the son of a Revolutionary War hero named Henry "Light Horse Harry" Lee. A graduate of West Point, Lee won fame when he captured abolitionist John Brown after his raid on Harpers Ferry. Although Lee was offered a position with the Union Army when the Civil War started, Lee could not accept.

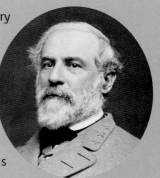

Robert E. Lee became general-in-chief of the Confederate Army in 1865.

Although he felt secession was wrong, he felt it was more wrong for the federal government to use force to preserve the Union—especially against Virginia, which he loved above all things. When Virginia left the Union, so did Lee.

September 17, 1862
The North declares victory in the Battle of Antietam.

September 22, 1862
President Lincoln issues the Emancipation Proclamation. This proclamation frees the slaves in most of the Confederacy.

Northern Army Life

Abraham Lincoln did not waste any time raising an army after Fort Sumter surrendered to the South Carolina militia. On April 15, 1861, Lincoln called on the governors of all the loyal Northern states to send 75,000 soldiers to Washington, D.C. Throughout the war, Lincoln would call for more volunteers every few months, with New York supplying more regiments than any other state in the North. Altogether, the Union fielded more than 2,100,000 soldiers, or about half its men of military age.

The Union had several ways to encourage men to join the army. One of the most popular ways was to pay a bounty, or cash reward, to any man who enlisted. Many recruits could earn as much as $677 in bounties from their local county, state, and the federal government. Some recruits made even more. By July 1864, a New York district was paying recruits a bounty of $1,060 apiece. One Illinois district advertised $1.055.95 a head. During the winter of 1864–65, enlistees at Philadelphia each received $1,100 in bounties. This was a lot of money in the 1860s—as much as two to three years' wages for common laborers—and enough to draw thousands of men into the army. However, bounties did not always work the way they were meant too. Many criminals joined the army as bounty jumpers. These men enlisted in the army, received their bounty money, and then deserted. Later, they would use a fake name to join a different army regiment and earn even more bounty money.

The Union also appealed to its citizens' patriotism to get them to join the army. Posters were hung in town squares and markets showing brave soldiers in battle defending their country. Newspaper advertisements carried the same message. Rallies and parades were held to cheer on regiments as they marched off to war. These activities created a patriotic feeling and a desire for adventure that convinced many men to join the army. However, it became harder and harder to find volunteers after the first year of the war.

Posters were just one of several ways the Union urged citizens to join the army.

November 5, 1862
Lincoln replaces McClellan as commander of the Army of the Potomac with Ambrose E. Burnside.

December 13, 1862
Robert E. Lee defeats Ambrose Burnside at the Battle of Fredericksburg, giving a major victory to the Confederacy.

Union Cavalry officers in Virginia, 1862.

In 1863, the U.S. Congress approved conscription, or drafting men into the army. This law was called the Enrollment Act, and it was actually designed to encourage enlistment. If you joined the army before you got a draft call, you would receive a cash bounty. If you waited to be drafted, there was no bounty.

Soldiers soon discovered that life in the army was not as adventurous or romantic as they had been told. Volunteers had to sleep outside, in all kinds of weather. They spent hours every day doing military drills and learning to use and care for their weapons. Disease also killed more soldiers than enemy soldiers did. A Union soldier stood twice the chance of dying from disease than enemy action, and a Rebel soldier, three times the chance.

Following the surrender of Fort Sumter, Lincoln was determined to preserve the Union and called on volunteers to fight.

Uniforms and Weaponry

The Northern states were full of factories that mass-produced uniforms, weapons, and ammunition for the troops. Most soldiers wore uniforms that included light blue pants, a dark blue coat or jacket, and a dark blue cap. In addition to weapons, infantry soldiers carried a knapsack made of painted canvas with leather straps that went over the shoulders and across the chest. This knapsack held the soldier's personal belongings. The soldier carried his food in a painted canvas haversack that hung on his left side with his canteen. His ammunition was carried in a black leather cartridge box that hung on his right hip. Some Union regiments wore different uniforms and colors.

At the start of the war, a .58-caliber rifle was the standard weapon for the Union Army. A gun's caliber was the size of the hole in the gun's muzzle, as well as the size of the bullets the gun fired. Many Union and Confederate soldiers also carried .577 Enfield rifle muskets imported from England.

Officers usually did not carry rifles. Instead, they carried swords. Many also bought revolvers for additional protection. Union cavalrymen carried sabers, revolvers, and short shoulder arms called "carbines." The standard weaponry for infantrymen was rifle muskets or rifles and also bayonets (a spike or sword attached to the muzzle of a rifle or rifle musket).

January 1, 1863
The Emancipation Proclamation goes into effect.

January 25, 1863
Lincoln names General Joseph Hooker as head of the Army of the Potomac, replacing General Burnside. Also on this date, the 54th Massachusetts Volunteer Infantry, the most famous black regiment, is authorized.

Southern Army Life

Like the Union, the Confederacy also relied on individual states to find soldiers at the beginning of the war. Later, these state soldiers were turned over to Confederate command. The Confederacy enlisted one-year volunteers in 1861, and then extended their enlistments to three years in April 1862. In February 1864, the Confederacy extended enlistments to the duration of the war.

North Carolina sent the largest number of army regiments in the Confederacy. During the early months of the war, Confederate

Confederate volunteers often wore a variety of uniforms.

Weaponry

Many soldiers arrived for duty carrying weapons from home or weapons given to them by state authorities, since, like their uniforms, weapons were also not standardized at the beginning of the war. The Confederate Army issued .58-caliber or .577-caliber rifles, similar to ones used in the North. Many of these weapons were seized from federal arsenals in the seceding states. By early 1863, the Confederate Army had imported more than 125,000 weapons from Europe. The rifles and muskets used in the Civil War had a longer range and were much more accurate than firearms carried in America's earlier major conflicts. This helped make the Civil War the bloodiest in American history. However, just as the limited number of factories in the South made it impossible to produce or replace uniforms on a large scale, it was hard to replace weapons, and find ammunition or replacement parts, as well.

Cannons were another powerful weapon on the battlefield. The most common cannon was the Model 1857 gun-howitzer. This cannon was often called the Napoleon, after the emperor of France, who had sponsored the development of the weapon. Cannons fired ammunition called shot. Some shot was round and some was pointed. Some was made of solid iron, and some contained explosive charges that detonated at desired ranges by cutting its fuse.

March 3, 1863
Lincoln signs the Enrollment Act, drafting men between the ages of twenty and forty-five.

"Stonewall" Jackson

May 1–4, 1863
Robert E. Lee defeats General Joseph Hooker at the Battle of Chancellorsville. It is a major Confederate victory, but the South loses one of its best commanders when General Thomas "Stonewall" Jackson is killed in battle.

president Jefferson Davis put out a call for volunteers every few months. Finally, in 1862, the Confederate government approved conscription. The Confederacy raised 800,000 to 900,000 troops, or about 80 to 90 percent of its total military manpower.

Like Union soldiers, the Confederate Army spent most of their time marching by day and camping outdoors at night. During the winter they lived in simple wooden barracks or cabins. During the rest of the year, they slept in tents or just lay down on the ground. Each soldier carried his own personal belongings. These belongings might have included a change of clothes, a tin plate and utensils for meals, Bibles, and pictures of loved ones left back home. When soldiers weren't practicing drills or repairing their equipment, they might have written letters home, read, played cards, gambled, or listened to concerts performed by army marching bands.

Uniforms

Southerners wore a variety of uniforms. At the beginning of the war, soldiers arrived wearing homemade uniforms often created by their wives or mothers. Many of these uniforms were very elaborate and included feathered plumes and colorful patterns. The South soon saw a need for a standard uniform, and army regulations called for an official Confederate uniform made of gray wool. The official uniform included pants, a high-collared jacket, and a cap called a kepi. The uniform was trimmed with blue and looked quite elegant. However, most soldiers did not wear this uniform because of supply problems. Instead, the typical Confederate infantryman wore a short jacket of gray or butternut, and gray, butternut, or light blue trousers. Like Union soldiers, a lot of Rebels favored broad-brimmed hats instead of visored caps for the additional sun protection. As the war went on, it became harder and harder to find a complete gray wool suit and it was close to impossible to replace such uniforms on a large scale. Many soldiers began wearing a uniform made of homespun cloth dyed brown with crushed butternuts. This uniform became so common that Southern soldiers were often called "Butternuts." Later in the war, Confederate soldiers were reduced to wearing rags or bits and pieces of different uniforms.

A soldier in uniform

May 14, 1863
Confederate troops abandon Jackson, Mississippi.

May 22, 1863
General Grant begins the siege of Vicksburg, Mississippi.

Black and Native American Soldiers and Women in the Army

In 1860, there were less than 500,000 free blacks in the United States, but there were almost four million black slaves. Could any of these men join the Union Army? At first, the answer was *no*. Although blacks were already serving in integrated crews in the U.S. Navy when the war began, even free blacks or escaped slaves living in the North were not allowed to join the army at first. This changed after President Lincoln issued the Emancipation Proclamation in 1863, which invited blacks to join the Union Army. About 179,000 black men took up the offer.

Black soldiers and sailors were not always treated equally when compared to white men. Only about 100 were allowed to become army officers. Black soldiers and sailors also faced a very special danger. If they were captured by the Confederate Army, they could be enslaved. Also, Confederate soldiers often refused to spare the lives of black prisoners, including helpless wounded men. Rebels also murdered many runaway slaves, including women and children.

The Emancipation Proclamation allowed former slaves to join the Union Army.

At first, black people were only allowed to do heavy labor or tasks behind the lines. Many white people believed that blacks would not be able to fight. They were especially doubtful that escaped slaves could be trained as soldiers because most slaves could not read or write. However, the soldiers soon proved them wrong. Soldiers who could not read simply memorized instructions and learned them through constant drilling. In addition, chaplains in black regiments taught reading and writing to the many soldiers who were eager to learn. Black soldiers were also just as brave and capable as white soldiers. Several black soldiers received the Medal of Honor, the highest award for bravery given by the Union.

One of about 179,000 volunteer black soldiers.

July 1–3, 1863
The North wins the Battle of Gettysburg, but more than 50,000 men are injured or killed.

Alexander Hamilton Stephens

July 2, 1863
Confederate Vice President Alexander Hamilton Stephens comes to Hampton Roads, Virginia, to discuss an end to the war, but Lincoln refuses his terms.

Native American Soldiers

Native Americans were a small but significant part of both the Union and the Confederate armies. The Confederacy began forming Indian regiments in Indian territory as early as 1861. An "Indian Brigade" composed of two regiments of Cherokees, Creeks, Seminoles, Chickasaws, Cherokees, Delawares, Kickapoos, Osage, Shawnees, and Senecas, was part of the Union Army that invaded Indian territory in the summer of 1862. However, many Confederate Indians deserted after the spring of 1862, and some ended up fighting for the Union. One of the most famous Native Americans was Stand Waite. Waite was a mixed-blood Cherokee political leader in Indian Territory (now Oklahoma). After the war started, he formed a regiment of Native Americans and went to fight for the Confederacy. Waite rose to the rank of brigadier general. In June 1865, he became the last Confederate general to surrender his troops. Waite was the only non-white general in the Civil War.

Although most did not fight on the battlefields, women were also an important part of the Union and Confederate armies. One of their most important roles was in hospitals. Women became nurses in large numbers during the Civil War. There were about 20,000 women nurses during the war, compared to 30,000 men nurses. These women were kept away from battlefield hospitals but were welcomed in town or city hospitals where the wounded were taken.

Women also served in other ways. Many sewed flags and bandages for army regiments. Also, in the North, many women were part of the Sanitary Commission. This organization brought medicine and supplies to the battlefield to aid soldiers. In addition, a large number of Northern women staffed federal offices in Washington, D.C., during the war.

Black soldiers of the 54th Massachusetts Regiment attack Fort Wagner, South Carolina (July 18, 1863).

Clara Barton
(1821–1912)

Clara Barton became one of the most famous nurses in the Civil War. Barton volunteered as a battlefield nurse in 1862. She was one of the few women to actually tend the wounded on the battlefield. Barton went on to start the American Red Cross.

Clara Barton, famous Civil War nurse and American Red Cross founder

Phoebe Pember
(1823–1913)

Phoebe Pember was another well-known nurse. She was called the "Confederate angel." Pember was a widow from South Carolina when she began volunteering in Confederate Army hospitals in and around Richmond, Virginia. She kept a journal of her experiences which was published after the war.

July 4, 1863
After a forty-day siege, Vicksburg, Mississippi, surrenders to Union forces and General Ulysses S. Grant captures a Rebel army of 30,000 men.

July 13–16, 1863
In response to the Enrollment Act, draft riots occur in several Northern cities, including New York and Boston.

September 19–20, 1863
At the Battle of Chickamauga, Confederates drive the Union Army back to Chattanooga, Tennessee.

The Naval War

The Civil War was not fought only on land. There were many battles on the water as well.

From the very first days of the war, when President Lincoln ordered a blockade of the Confederate coast, the navy was an important part of the war effort. Union sailors blockaded many Southern seaports to prevent weapons, food, medicine, and other supplies from reaching the soldiers nearby. Both the Union and Confederacy used ships to transport soldiers and supplies across rivers and lakes. Both sides also found ships by converting existing vessels into warships, or building and buying new ships. The Union Navy was quick to establish its domination of inland waterways, which greatly helped the Union Army conquer the Confederacy.

The Confederacy used mines to protect its waters.

Merchant Ships

The naval war was also fought against merchant ships. These ships carried goods from one part of the United States to another, and to and from the United States and Europe. Merchant ships were often targeted by the opposing navy, which attacked the usually unarmed ships and stole their cargo.

In addition to ironclad ships, the Confederacy came up with another clever way to protect its waters. It used mines called torpedoes. These mines floated just below the surface of the water and could sink or damage any ship that crossed their paths. Mines were usually wooden or tin containers filled with explosives. When a passing ship hit the mine, it exploded. These mines were very effective. They also caused an international outcry. Many other nations felt that using submerged mines was cowardly and also claimed that mines violated the rules of warfare. The Confederacy didn't care—it went right on using them.

Semisubmersibles were another Southern naval weapon. These crafts rode so low in the water than only the tops were visible. Semisubmersibles carried an explosive mounted on a wooden beam. This beam could be rammed into the side of a ship, setting off the explosive and sinking the enemy vessel. Semisubmersibles usually operated at night, when darkness made it even harder to see the underwater danger.

November 19, 1863
President Lincoln delivers his historic Gettysburg Address.

November 23–25, 1863
General Grant drives the Confederate Army of Tennessee out of Chattanooga; the Confederates abandon Knoxville, leaving all of Tennessee under Union control.

During the war Confederate mines, like these in the Potomac River, could sink or damage any ship.

The *Monitor* vs. the *Virginia*

The most famous naval battle of the war occurred in 1862 when the *Monitor* and the *Virginia* faced each other. The *Virginia* started out as a wooden ship but was changed into a Confederate ironclad warship in 1861. When the Union Navy heard about this, it rushed to build its own ironclad ship, the *Monitor*. The *Monitor* came to defend the Union ships, and the two ironclads met on March 9, 1862. However, the battle did not amount to much. Since both ships were covered with iron, cannonballs simply bounced off the sides. No one was killed or seriously injured, and neither side won the battle. Still, the confrontation made it clear that ironclad ships were much better protected than wooden ships. Soon, wooden warships all over the world were considered out of date and were replaced by ironclad vessels.

Any sailor who served in the navy could be put in danger. Many were killed or injured by bullets, cannonballs, or bits of flying iron or wood from explosions. Many more were killed when boilers exploded and scalded them with hot water or steam. However, serving onboard a ship was much safer than fighting a battle on land. Out of 132,000 sailors in the Union Navy, only 1,804 were killed during the war.

The Monitor *met the* Virginia *on March 9, 1862.*

Inside the gun turret of the Monitor, *an ironclad ship the Union Navy built*

March 10, 1864
General Grant is named commander of all the Union armies.

May 4, 1864
General Sherman begins his march toward the Confederate capital of Richmond, Virginia.

May 5–6, 1864
Lee and Grant face each other at the Battle of the Wilderness in Virginia.

Spies and Rangers

Every war has had its share of spies. There have always been people who have aided one side or the other by passing along secret information or who have worked to defeat the enemy other than in battle. The Civil War was no exception.

Some of the most famous Civil War spies were women. Elizabeth Van Lew was a resident of Virginia who became a spy for the North. Van Lew was a member of an important family in Richmond, the capital of the Confederacy, but she believed strongly in the Union. Van Lew pretended to be mentally ill so

Elizabeth Van Lew, a Civil War spy known as "Crazy Bet"

Elizabeth Van Lew at home with her nieces, brother John, and servant.

that Confederate leaders who visited her family would not take her seriously. The trick worked, and she became known as "Crazy Bet." However, Van Lew was only pretending to be crazy. When Confederate leaders spoke freely of their plans, Van Lew listened to every word. Then she used messengers to send the information

May 8–12, 1864
Lee and Grant's armies meet again at the Battle of Spotsylvania in Virginia, but neither side gains a clear victory.

The Battle of Spotsylvania

to contacts in the Union. Van Lew's information was so helpful that after the war ended, General Ulysses S. Grant personally thanked her for her help.

Other spies were members of the army. Henry T. Harrison was a Confederate army officer. He was also a scout and a spy. Harrison pinpointed Union army positions before the Battle of Gettysburg, which helped Confederate General Robert E. Lee during the battle.

Many spies got away with their work. Others were caught, imprisoned, and even killed. Spying was a dangerous way to help the cause, but many people took part in these efforts to do their part.

PARTISAN RANGERS

A group called the Partisan Rangers were another important weapon. In 1862, the Confederacy passed the Partisan Ranger Act. This law allowed people who weren't soldiers to band together and attack the enemy's men, supplies, and weapons.

The most famous Partisan Ranger was John Singleton Mosby. At the start of the war, Mosby was a lawyer in Virginia. He quickly became a Partisan Ranger. He organized about 800 other Rangers during the war. Working in smaller groups, these Rangers crept out at night to destroy railroad tracks and bridges so that supplies could not get through to the Union army. Mosby's men also attacked by day, hitting Union army camps, capturing officers, and stealing property from supply trains. Mosby then sold this property to the Confederacy, so the South would have more ammunition and other supplies. He was so sneaky and successful that he became known as the "Gray Ghost." The Union was desperate to capture Mosby, but although he was wounded seven times, Mosby was never captured. General Robert E. Lee called him one of his most valuable men.

John Mosby, famous Partisan Ranger who became known as the "Gray Ghost"

June 7, 1864
Republicans nominate Abraham Lincoln for a second term as president, along with vice presidential candidate Andrew Johnson, a senator from Tennessee who had remained loyal to the Union.

Bull Run and Other Major Battles

THE BATTLE OF BULL RUN

The Civil War was marked by a number of important battles. One of the first major battles was called the Battle of Bull Run by the North because it was fought at a small creek in Virginia called Bull Run. The South called this battle Manassas after a nearby railroad junction. Whatever the name, the battle would be one of the strangest and most horrifying of the war.

The First Battle of Bull Run, one of the first major battles

The Battle of Bull Run took place on July 21, 1861. Many Northerners thought this would be the only battle of the war. They expected the North to defeat the South so overwhelmingly that the war would end right there. To them, the battle was a spectator sport. Hundreds of people, including many women dressed in their finest party clothes, gathered on a nearby hill to picnic and watch the battle. They got more than they expected.

The Confederate army, led by General P.G.T. Beauregard, had 22,000 men. Another Confederate, Joseph E. Johnston, was able to bring Beauregard about 8,500 to 9,000 reinforcements from the Shenandoah Valley in time to help fight in this battle. They faced 30,000 Union soldiers led by Brigadier General Irvin McDowell. Both armies were poorly trained, and neither could defeat the other. Then, in mid-afternoon, Beauregard's army received more soldiers. The increased numbers allowed them to drive the Union Army from the field. The people watching from the hill got so frightened that they ran away, blocking the roads away from the battlefield. This panicked the Union soldiers, and they dropped their weapons and ran, too. In the end, a total of 1,205 men were killed and more than 2,500 were wounded on both sides. The Confederates captured 1,200 Union soldiers. It was clear to everyone that the South was stronger than expected and that the war would be far longer and bloodier than anyone believed.

June 15, 1864
The siege of Petersburg, Virginia, by the Union Army begins.

June 27, 1864
Confederate troops under General Joseph Johnston win a big victory over General Sherman at the Battle of Kenesaw Mountain in Georgia.

July 17, 1864
Confederate President Davis replaces General Joseph Johnston with General John B. Hood because Davis is impatient at Johnston's inability to halt Sherman's march to Atlanta.

THE SECOND BATTLE OF BULL RUN

One year later, on August 28–30, 1862, the North and South met again at Bull Run. This time, the Northern Army was led by General John Pope. Pope was no match for the Confederate Army led by Robert E. Lee. Even though the South had a little over half the number of men Pope had, it soundly defeated the North. Soon afterward, Pope was transferred to the West and most of his troops joined General McClellan's army.

THE BATTLE OF ANTIETAM

Antietam was another important battle. This battle was fought on September 17, 1862, along Antietam Creek near Sharpsburg, Maryland. Sharpsburg was just forty miles from Washington, D.C., and many Northerners were alarmed by this invasion of Northern territory. General Robert E. Lee was the Confederate commander, and General McClellan was the Union leader sent to stop him.

The two armies fought for fourteen hours, with more than 100,000 men in the field. When the battle finally ended, more than 23,000 men were dead or injured, making this the bloodiest single day of the war. McClellan did not destroy Lee's army, but he did force it back to Virginia. The North claimed the victory because it had stopped Lee's march north and ended its invasion of the Union states.

By the end of Antietam, McClellan forced Lee's army back to Virginia.

The Battle of Antietam was the bloodiest single day of the war.

After the Battle of Antietam, more than 23,000 men were dead or injured.

General Joseph Johnston

July 20–28, 1864
General Hood attacks General Sherman outside Atlanta but suffers heavy losses; General Sherman continues his march toward Atlanta.

August 5, 1864
Union naval Admiral David G. Farragut moves into Mobile Bay, an important Confederate port in Alabama.

The Emancipation Proclamation

On September 22, 1862, just five days after the Battle of Antietam, President Abraham Lincoln issued his Emancipation Proclamation. The document stated: "On the first day of January, in the year of our Lord one thousand eight hundred and sixty three, all persons held as slaves within any State, or designated part of a State, the people whereof shall then be in rebellion against the United States, shall be then, thenceforth, and forever free." In simple words, Lincoln declared the slaves living in most of the Confederacy to be free.

Lincoln's proclamation was a decisive moment in American history.

Lincoln's proclamation was bold, but it actually did not change much. The proclamation didn't have any effect in the North, because slavery in those states was already illegal. It also did not apply to Southern states that did not secede from the Union: Maryland, Kentucky, Missouri, and Delaware. The only slaves covered by the Emancipation Proclamation were in the Confederacy, and the Confederate government did not recognize Lincoln's authority. Therefore, no Southern slave owners actually freed any slaves as a result of the proclamation.

However, the proclamation was a decisive moment in American history. The federal government had taken the first step toward destroying slavery. Every Union military advance would free slaves. If slavery was outlawed in the Confederate states, it could not survive in the rest of the South because it would be too easy for the remaining slaves to run away to free territory.

In addition, the Emancipation Proclamation did allow former slaves to join the Union army. By the end of the war, about 179,000 black soldiers had taken up arms against the South.

The Emancipation Proclamation was not totally popular in the Northern states. Many soldiers had joined the Union Army out of patriotism or a desire to keep the United States together, not to

August 29, 1864
Democrats nominate George McClellan to run against Abraham Lincoln for president.

A devastated section of Atlanta

free black slaves. Lincoln's proclamation put a whole new perspective on the war. Many abolitionists cheered the proclamation, but were disappointed that it did not actually free all slaves. However, most white Northerners came to accept the Proclamation because it weakened the Confederacy.

In spite of public feeling and the realities of slavery, the Emancipation Proclamation did help change the tide of the war. The real power of the proclamation was political and moral. It was now clear that a Northern victory in the Civil War would not just put a broken nation back together. It would also ensure that freedom would apply to all.

The Emancipation Proclamation also helped win the support of other nations. Now that there was a moral side to the conflict, it was easier for Great Britain, France, and other European nations which had outlawed slavery to refuse to help the Confederacy. Lincoln clearly understood the importance of the proclamation. Before he signed it, he said, "If my name ever goes into history it will be for this act, and my whole soul is in it."

The Emancipation Proclamation

By the President of the United States of America:

A Proclamation.

Whereas, on the twenty-second day of September, in the year of our Lord one thousand eight hundred and sixty-two, a proclamation was issued by the President of the United States, containing, among other things, the following, to wit:

"That on the first day of January, in the "year of our Lord one thousand eight hundred "and sixty-three, all persons held as slaves within "any State or designated part of a State, the people "whereof shall then be in rebellion against the "United States, shall be then, thenceforward, and "forever free; and the Executive Government of the "United States, including the military and naval "authority thereof, will recognize and maintain "the freedom of such persons, and will do no act "or acts to repress such persons, or any of them, "in any efforts they may make for their actual "freedom.

"That the Executive will, on the first day

September 2, 1864
Atlanta falls to General Sherman and his Union forces.

November 8, 1864
Abraham Lincoln is re-elected president.

November 15, 1864
General Sherman begins his March to the Sea in Georgia.

Gettysburg and the Gettysburg Address

Gettysburg was the most famous battle of the Civil War. It was fought in a small town in Pennsylvania. The battle was the bloodiest of the war, and also an important turning point for the North.

During the summer of 1863, Confederate troops under Robert E. Lee were again pushing toward the North. Their goal was to invade western Pennsylvania and then turn east toward the major cities of Philadelphia, New York, and the nation's capital of Washington, D.C. Lee's plan was to relieve the strained Virginia countryside by moving the war north, disrupt Union economic security east of the Susquehanna River, damage Northern morale, and finally win British and French recognition for the Confederacy. Gettysburg, Pennsylvania was on this route.

In late June, Lee led his army of 75,000 men toward Gettysburg. He knew Union troops were in the area, but he did not know how many. He certainly did not expect the more than 88,000 Union soldiers who were marching to town under the leadership of Major General George G. Meade.

On July 1, 1863, the two huge armies met. The fighting lasted until July 3 and included several smaller battles in the fields and woods around Gettysburg. These battles took the names of where they were fought: Cemetery Hill, Little Round Top, Culp's Hill, McPherson's Ridge, Devil's Den, and the Wheat Field. At first, the Southern troops moved along the sides of the strong Northern Army, looking for a break in the lines. Meanwhile, the North blasted the Confederates with gunfire and cannon fire from a strong central position. Finally, on July 3, the Confederates charged the Union directly. This attack was called Pickett's Charge after George E. Pickett, who helped lead the attack. So many soldiers were killed or injured at Gettysburg that streams ran red with their blood. When the fighting finally stopped, more than 50,000 men were dead or injured.

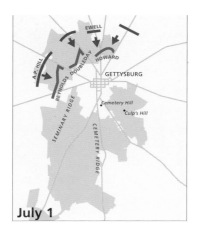

July 1

The Union and Confederate armies met and battled.

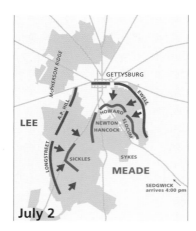

July 2

Fighting continued through the second day.

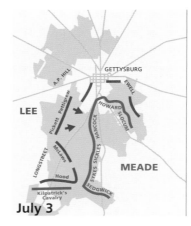

July 3

Pickett's Charge occurred and the battles finally ended.

November 30, 1864
Confederate General Hood attacks a Union army in the Battle of Franklin in Tennessee. Hood is badly beaten and loses six of his generals.

Tennessee

December 21, 1864
General Sherman captures Savannah, Georgia, and presents it to President Lincoln as a Christmas gift.

Lee's army did a tremendous amount of damage to Meade's troops. However, the Southern army suffered even more. Lee lost more than a third of his men—28,000 out of 75,000—while Meade lost about a quarter. "It has been a sad, sad day to us," Lee said later. He offered to resign from the army, but Confederate President Jefferson Davis refused.

THE GETTYSBURG ADDRESS

The total number of dead and injured at Gettysburg added up to about 28,000 Southerners and 23,000 Northerners. In the months afterward, Gettysburg was filled with wounded soldiers being cared for in makeshift hospitals. A military cemetery was built near the town's graveyard on Cemetery Hill to hold all the dead, and their bodies were arranged by their home states. President Lincoln was invited to speak at the cemetery's dedication on November 19, 1863. His remarks became known as the Gettysburg Address.

Lincoln spoke for only a little more than two minutes, but his remarks are considered to be one of the greatest speeches ever

Abraham Lincoln's Gettysburg Address is considered to be one of the greatest speeches ever given.

A draft of President Lincoln's Gettysburg Address.

given. Among his words, Lincoln said, "The world will little note, nor long remember what we say here, but it can never forget what they did here. . . . We here highly resolve that these dead shall not have died in vain—that this nation, under God, shall have a new birth of freedom—and that government of the people, by the people, for the people, shall not perish from the earth."

Janaury 1865
General Sherman issues an order granting abandoned land in Florida, Georgia, and South Carolina to freed black slaves. Each family is promised forty acres, a mule, farm equipment, and seeds.

January 31, 1865
The House of Representatives passes the Thirteenth Amendment, outlawing slavery.

The Siege of Vicksburg and the Fall of Atlanta

Although General Lee had moved the war out of Virginia for a time, it continued to rage in many parts of the South. As Northern troops moved deeper and deeper into the South, they caused tremendous destruction.

THE SIEGE OF VICKSBURG

Vicksburg, Mississippi, was a town that sat on high ground overlooking the Mississippi River. Its location between Memphis, Tennessee and New Orleans, Louisiana, made it very important, since the river was a major route of transportation for the Confederates. The town became even more important after the Union Navy gained control of Memphis and New Orleans in 1862. Now Vicksburg was the only place where the Confederacy could ship goods from west to east across the Mississippi River. The South surrounded the town with heavy cannons and fortifications to keep any enemy ships and troops away.

General Ulysses S. Grant was commanding the Army of the Tennessee during the Vicksburg campaign. He made several attempts to conquer Vicksburg, but each one failed. Then, in May 1863, Grant tried again. By crossing the Mississippi River south of

In 1863 at the Siege of Vicksburg, Grant commanded Union forces.

Vicksburg and attacking the town from the rear, he was able to drive Confederate defenders into the town itself. Then Grant surrounded Vicksburg. Meanwhile, the Union Navy fired artillery shells on Vicksburg's defenses.

For forty days, Vicksburg was cut off from the rest of the South and under constant attack by Union forces. General John C. Pemberton tried to defend Vicksburg, but there was little he could do to break the siege. The people of the city dug bomb shelters into the hills for protection. Finally, knowing soldiers and residents were exhausted, starving, and unable to defend themselves any longer, Pemberton surrendered to Grant on July 4, 1863. About 30,000 Rebel soldiers surrendered to Grant that day.

February 1, 1865
Illinois becomes the first state to ratify, or approve, the Thirteenth Amendment, which will make slavery unconstitutional everywhere in the United States.

February 22, 1865
Wilmington, North Carolina, the last open Confederate port, falls to Union forces.

The South used cannons in their defenses during the Siege of Vicksburg.

Grant marched into the town just one day after the Union's victory at the Battle of Gettysburg. The two victories made it clear that the South was weakening.

THE FALL OF ATLANTA

Next, the Union set their sights on Atlanta, Georgia. Atlanta was one of the largest cities in the South, and an important railroad center. Without the supplies moving out of Atlanta, the South might have been defeated much earlier. In 1864, Major General William Tecumseh Sherman assembled 100,000 men and marched on Atlanta. It took him more than two months to fight his way from Tennessee into the city. Finally, on July 18–19, 1864, Sherman came within fifteen miles of the city. General John B. Hood, who was protecting Atlanta, failed to drive him away and only weakened his own army in these attacks. Fighting continued around the city until September 2, when Hood withdrew his army and Atlanta finally surrendered. Sherman's men destroyed all the military facilities in Atlanta. They also burned most of the city and ripped up the railroad tracks.

THE BATTLE OF SPOTSYLVANIA

During the spring of 1864, the North continued to pound away at the South. Still, the South was not ready to give up. In May 1864, General Lee's Confederate forces held back Grant's advance at an important battle at Spotsylvania Court House near Fredericksburg, Virginia.

The Union Army's leader, General Grant, was headed to Richmond, Virginia, the Confederate capital, but Lee's army stood in his way. When the two met, Lee defeated Grant. Although 12,000 Southern soldiers were killed or wounded, including prisoners—about half of the Union's casualties—it was harder for Lee to replace them. Lee had won the battle, but his army never fully recovered its strength.

Battle at Spotsylvania Court House near Fredericksburg, Virginia, May 1864

March 3, 1865
Congress establishes the Bureau of Refugees, Freedmen, and Abandoned Lands, better known as the Freedmen's Bureau.

Sherman's March to the Sea

General Sherman did not stop at Atlanta. He wanted to split the Confederacy in half for the second time and show the people of the Confederacy that their army was no longer able to defend them. Sherman said, "If we can march a well-appointed army right through Jefferson Davis' territory, it is a demonstration to the world, foreign and domestic, that we have a power which Davis cannot resist." General Ulysses S. Grant agreed and gave Sherman permission to march through Georgia to the Atlantic Ocean.

The army carried few supplies. Instead, Sherman ordered his men to live off the land. The army found plenty to eat in the plantations and fields of Georgia. They gathered crops and killed animals along the way, adding to the devastation of the South. They also destroyed anything that might have any value to the Confederacy, including livestock, wagons, railroads, and supply centers. Their actions showed Sherman's belief in total war. He believed that defeating the South's armies was not enough. Instead, the Union had to destroy anything that would help the South make war. "We are not only fighting hostile enemies, but a hostile people," Sherman said, "and must make old and young, rich and poor, feel the hard hand of war."

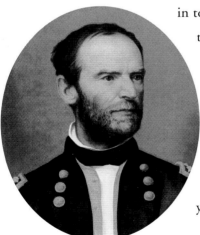

General William T. Sherman

The Union destroyed anything of value to the Confederacy, like railroads and supply centers.

Sherman reached the outskirts of Savannah on December 10. A Confederate force led by General William J. Hardee was no match for him. After only a fifteen-minute fight on December 21, Hardee and his army abandoned Savannah. Sherman marched through Savannah in a victory parade. Then, the general sent a telegram to Lincoln, giving him the city of Savannah as a Christmas gift.

March 4, 1865
Lincoln is inaugurated for his second term as president.

April 2, 1865
The Confederate capital, Richmond, Virginia, is captured by the Union; Petersburg, Virginia, falls to the Union after a nine-month-long siege.

April 9, 1865
Confederate General Robert E. Lee surrenders his army to Union General Ulysses S. Grant at Appomattox Court House, Virginia, signifying the end of the Civil War.

A devastated section of Atlanta

Unlike Atlanta, Sherman and his men did not destroy Savannah. Instead, they used it as a base and later marched north into South Carolina, where they caused even more destruction. Sherman had achieved his goal of cutting the Confederacy in half. He showed the world that the Union was too powerful for the South, and that the Confederacy had become what he called "a hollow shell."

"March to the Sea"

Sherman's march through the Confederacy is called the "March to the Sea." It began on November 15, 1864, when Sherman led 62,000 men out of Atlanta. The army headed east toward Savannah, Georgia, spreading out over an area between 25 to 60 miles wide as they marched.

April 12, 1865
Mobile falls to the Union Army after a siege.

April 14, 1865
President Lincoln is shot by John Wilkes Booth while attending a play in Washington, D.C.

Hospitals, Prisoners, and Refugees

Tens of thousands of soldiers were wounded during the Civil War. Injured soldiers were carried behind the battle lines and loaded onto crude ambulances. These ambulances were nothing more than horse-drawn carriages, so the bumpy ride to the field hospital was agonizing for wounded soldiers.

The worst injuries were treated at hospitals near the battlefields. However, there were few options available to treat war wounds. Rifles fired heavy, powerful bullets that smashed bones and shredded flesh. It was often impossible for doctors to repair

Hospitals near battlefields treated the worst injuries.

these injuries, so they usually ended up amputating the damaged limb. Amputations were the most common operation in an army hospital, and thousands of men lost an arm or a leg during the war.

Civil War surgery was nothing like surgery today. For one thing, there were no good anesthetics. Some surgeons used chemicals called ether or chloroform to knock a patient unconscious, but anesthetic supplies were limited and many soldiers went under the knife without any painkillers. Surgeons learned to work fast and cut off the damaged limb as quickly as possible to lessen the pain of the operation. Speed was also important because a prolonged amputation would lead to the fatal onset of shock. A trained military surgeon could remove the limb in 90 seconds. If the patient recovered from such a serious injury, he was sent home with an honorable discharge from the army. Other patients were sent to hospitals in nearby cities and were cared for by nurses or volunteers until they were well enough to go home.

Even after surgery, a patient was still in danger. There were no antibiotics or other drugs to fight infection, and most battle and surgical wounds became infected. Thousands more soldiers died from disease. Illnesses such as cholera, diphtheria, dysentery, malaria, yellow fever, and measles spread quickly in crowded army camps and could kill a large number of soldiers in an incredibly short period of time. For every Union soldier killed on the battlefield, two more died of disease. The rate was three to one in the Confederate Army.

April 15, 1865
President Lincoln dies; Andrew Johnson becomes president.

April 26, 1865
John Wilkes Booth is shot and killed by a Union cavalryman.

The Confederate prison at Andersonville, Georgia

Andersonville Prison

The most notorious prison was the Confederate prison at Andersonville, Georgia. This prison held 40,000 men—about four times the amount it was built to handle. Each prisoner had a living space of only six by six feet. The only shelter was shabby tents or huts the prisoners built out of scraps of wood. Neither provided much protection from the hot weather or the swarms of insects. During the hottest part of the summer, more than one hundred prisoners died every day. By the end of the war, 13,000 men had died at Andersonville.

If hospitals were a bad place for a soldier to be, a prison could be even worse. It is estimated that 144,000 Union soldiers ended up in Confederate prisoner-of-war camps during the Civil War, while 214,000 Confederates were held in the North. These soldiers often had poor food and even worse sanitation. Diseases such as dysentery and other infections spread quickly, killing thousands of men. About 30,000 Union prisoners died during the war, along with 26,000 Confederates.

Refugees were another sad casualty of the war. Most refugees were women and children, left behind when their husbands, fathers, and brothers went off to fight. Many men were displaced as well. Some were too old to fight. Others stayed with their families to try to protect them. When an opposing army passed through an area, they often chased people from their homes. Other people became refugees when armies burned houses or entire towns, or destroyed livestock and crops, leaving people with nothing to eat. While some refugees were able to get money from the government to start

13,000 prisoners had died at Andersonville by the end of the war.

over, most were on their own. After the war, there was little to return to, as most found their homes destroyed by fire or violence. Runaway and freed slaves also made up a large portion of the refugee population.

May 13, 1865
The last battle of the Civil War is fought on the Rio Grande in Texas at Palmito Ranch, where Confederate cavalry defeat a Union force.

May 1865
The remaining Confederate troops surrender.

November 1865
Ulysses S. Grant tours the South and recommends a gentle Reconstruction policy.

December 6, 1865
The Thirteenth Amendment goes into effect.

The Surrender at Appomattox

By 1865, it was clear that the South could not win the war. The last months of the war saw the surrender and destruction of many Southern cities, including Petersburg, Virginia; Charleston, South Carolina; Columbia, South Carolina; and Raleigh, North Carolina. When the Confederate capital city, Richmond, Virginia, fell on April 2, 1865, President Jefferson Davis and General Robert E. Lee knew the end was very near.

Lee and his army fled Richmond and tried to move into North Carolina to join up with another Confederate force, but they could not escape the Union Army. Instead, Lee retreated to the west. By April 8, he was surrounded in the town of Appomattox Court House, Virginia.

Lee met with Union General Grant in a private house in the town on April 9, 1865. There, Lee surrendered his army.

Federal soldiers at Appomattox Court House, Virginia

April 1866
Civil Rights Act is passed, giving black men citizenship and the same rights as white citizens.

July 1866
Congress expands the responsibilities and powers of the Freedmen's Bureau; Tennessee becomes the first Confederate state to be readmitted to the Union.

Miss Cooke's School room, the Freedmen's Bureau, Richmond, VA

Lee met with Grant and surrendered his army on April 9, 1865.

Grant was generous to Lee and his men. He gave Southern troops food, which they badly needed. Grant also paroled all the soldiers when they surrendered. This meant they were allowed to go home and none would be arrested for treason against the United States. In addition, Grant agreed to Lee's request that his troops keep their horses, since the men had owned them before the war. Officers were also allowed to keep their weapons, which they had purchased themselves.

Most Southern soldiers were relieved that the war was finally over. N. Albert Sherman, a Union soldier who witnessed Lee's surrender, wrote that after the ceremony he "had a chat with our Southern brethren most of whom were glad of the doings of the day." However, these Confederate soldiers faced a grim reality as they headed home. Most had to walk back to their farms or hometowns because the railroads had been destroyed during the war. As

they walked through scenes of abandonment and destruction, they must have dreaded what would be waiting for them when they came home. For most, their farms had been destroyed or neglected so badly that they had to be completely rebuilt.

Most Wanted

After Lee's surrender, the most wanted man in the South was Confederate President Jefferson Davis. He had escaped from Richmond after the city fell on April 2 and was not seen for several weeks. Finally, he was captured in Georgia on May 10. Davis spent two years in military custody in a dungeon-like prison in Fort Monroe, Virginia. Finally, in May 1867, he was bailed out of prison by a group of Northern and Southern public figures, including a Northern newspaper publisher named Horace Greeley. Davis spent several years writing his memoirs, which was published in 1881. Davis refused to beg pardon for leading the rebellion and defended his conduct until he died in 1889.

A Northern print shows Jefferson Davis being captured while dressed as a woman.

March 1867
Congress passes the First Reconstruction Act, which divides the South into military districts.

May 16, 1868
President Andrew Johnson is impeached but escapes conviction by just one vote and remains president.

Lincoln's Assassination

President Lincoln and the federal government rejoiced at Lee's surrender and the end of the war. However, their joy did not last long.

On April 14, 1865, Lincoln, his wife, and two friends went to see the play *Our American Cousin* at Ford's Theatre in Washington, D.C. For Lincoln, it was a rare night out and a chance to relax and enjoy himself, before he made plans to integrate the defeated South back into the United States. About 10:30 that night, in the middle of the play, a Southerner named John Wilkes Booth slipped into the box where the president was sitting. Booth was an actor and was from a famous theatrical family. He was also a strong supporter of slavery and the Confederacy. Booth considered Lincoln a tyrant and blamed him for the South's defeat. "Our country owed all our troubles to Lincoln," Booth wrote.

At Ford's Theatre on April 14, 1865, Booth assassinated Lincoln and escaped.

July 28, 1868
The Fourteenth Amendment confirms the Civil Rights Act of 1866 by making African Americans U. S. citizens and citizens of any state they choose as home.

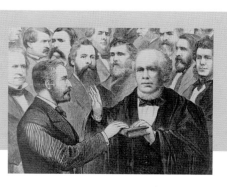

1869
Ulysses S. Grant is inaugurated as president.

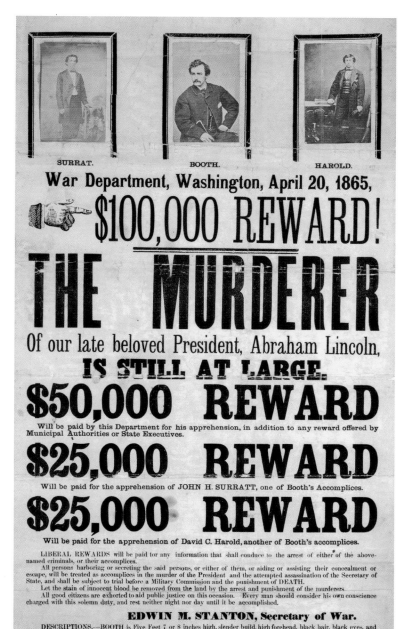

SURRAT.   BOOTH.   HAROLD.

War Department, Washington, April 20, 1865,

$100,000 REWARD!

THE MURDERER

Of our late beloved President, Abraham Lincoln,
IS STILL AT LARGE.

$50,000 REWARD

Will be paid by this Department for his apprehension, in addition to any reward offered by Municipal Authorities or State Executives.

$25,000 REWARD

Will be paid for the apprehension of JOHN H. SURRATT, one of Booth's Accomplices.

$25,000 REWARD

Will be paid for the apprehension of David C. Harold, another of Booth's accomplices.

LIBERAL REWARDS will be paid for any information that shall conduce to the arrest of either of the above-named criminals, or their accomplices.

All persons harboring or secreting the said persons, or either of them, or aiding or assisting their concealment or escape, will be treated as accomplices in the murder of the President and the attempted assassination of the Secretary of State, and shall be subject to trial before a Military Commission and the punishment of DEATH.

Let the stain of innocent blood be removed from the land by the arrest and punishment of the murderers.

All good citizens are exhorted to aid public justice on this occasion. Every man should consider his own conscience charged with this solemn duty, and rest neither night nor day until it be accomplished.

EDWIN M. STANTON, Secretary of War.

DESCRIPTIONS.—BOOTH is Five Feet 7 or 8 inches high, slender build, high forehead, black hair, black eyes, and wears a heavy black moustache.

JOHN H. SURRAT is about 5 feet, 9 inches. Hair rather thin and dark; eyes rather light; no beard. Would weigh 145 or 150 pounds. Complexion rather pale and clear, with color in his cheeks. Wore light clothes of fine quality. Shoulders square; cheek bones rather prominent; chin narrow; ears projecting at the top; forehead rather low and square, but broad. Parts his hair on the right side; neck rather long. His lips are firmly set. A slim man.

DAVID C. HAROLD is five feet six inches high, hair dark, eyes dark, eyebrows rather heavy, full face, nose short, hand short and fleshy, feet small, instep high, round bodied, naturally quick and active, slightly closes his eyes when looking at a person.

NOTICE.—In addition to the above, State and other authorities have offered rewards amounting to almost one hundred thousand dollars, making an aggregate of about TWO HUNDRED THOUSAND DOLLARS.

Posters advertised a reward for the capture of the President's murderer.

When Booth slipped into Lincoln's box, he pulled out a gun and shot the president in the back of the head. Booth then jumped down to the stage, yelling in Latin, "Thus shall it ever be for tyrants." He broke his leg in the fall, but managed to escape on horseback. A week later, Booth was trapped in a farmhouse in Virginia by Union cavalry and shot to death.

John Wilkes Booth

At first, people thought the gunshot and Booth's startling appearance were part of the play. Then someone screamed, "The president has been shot." Lincoln was carried to a house across the street. He remained unconscious through the night and died at 7:22 the next morning. The nation, already weary after four years of war, was devastated and frightened by Lincoln's death. Lincoln was the first U.S. president to be assassinated. A Union soldier, Sergeant Lucius Barber, wrote that the United States had been "plunged into the deepest sorrow by the most brutal murder of its loved chief."

After Lincoln's assassination, Vice President Andrew Johnson became the leader of the newly reunited nation. Johnson was from Tennessee, a Confederate state, and the only member of the Senate from a seceded state to remain loyal to the Union. Many Southerners and Northerners did not trust him. Johnson knew he had a difficult job ahead of him.

After Lincoln's assassination, Andrew Johnson became the new national leader.

February 1870

Hiram Revels becomes the first black U.S. senator. He serves until March 4, 1871, to occupy Jefferson Davis' old seat; the 15th Amendment is ratified, giving the right to vote to all male citizens, regardless of color.

The End of the War

The South was a mess after the Civil War. For more than ten years after the war ended, federal troops occupied some parts of the South. This period was called Reconstruction. President Lincoln came up with this term to describe a process where a loyal civilian government would be restored in the former Confederacy. Before the war's end, he specified that would involve acceptance that slavery was forever outlawed. After his death, Radical Republicans attempted to expand Reconstruction into an effort to grant Southern blacks political equality.

Carpetbaggers came to the South for various reasons.

The South faced many challenges. The first was in government. During Reconstruction, no candidate could run for office in the South without the approval of federal officials. For a time, former Confederate officials were not allowed to hold public office at all.

Many dishonest people took advantage of the chaotic political system in the post-war South. Men came to the South from other areas and were often elected to local governments. These men were called carpetbaggers for the cheap type of luggage their political enemies claimed they carried. Carpetbaggers were hated by most former Confederates, who viewed them as outsiders trying to take over the South. However, some Southerners cooperated with carpetbaggers. These men became known as scalawags, an insulting term.

Although some carpetbaggers did come to the South to take advantage of a bad situation, most came for different reasons. Many carpetbaggers were Northerners who came south in search of economic opportunities for themselves. They invested a lot of their own money in the South and got many of their friends to do the same. This contributed enormously to the South's economic recovery. Some carpetbaggers were former Union Army officers who fell in love with the South during the war. Some, like Governor Powell Clayton of Arkansas, married Southern women and started families in the South.

Former Confederate soldiers had to swear an oath of allegiance to the United States in order to be

July 15, 1870
Georgia becomes the last Confederate state to be readmitted to the Union.

Georgia

1872
The Freedmen's Bureau is abolished; Grant is re-elected president.

treated as full citizens again, and some veterans never did regain all of their rights, including the right to vote. The South also faced the task of rebuilding its economy. It had to start almost from scratch and build a new economy that was not based on plantations and the cheap labor provided by slaves.

Perhaps the South's greatest challenge was integrating millions of newly freed slaves into a life of freedom. Some of these freed slaves left the South altogether and looked for new opportunities in the North. However, most stayed behind and tried to build new lives.

Former slaves were encouraged to vote in local elections and help build a new leadership in the South. Thanks to the Reconstruction laws and the 14th Amendment, blacks were also

Jefferson Davis looking on as Revels filled his seat in the U. S. Senate.

able to participate in national elections. Many were elected to Southern state legislatures and some even served briefly in the U.S. Congress. Hiram Revels, a black man from Mississippi, was elected to fill Jefferson Davis' seat in the U.S. Senate. Although things seemed promising for African Americans in the South for a while, after federal troops left, these blacks quickly faced the reality of prejudice and inequality.

Hiram Revels and other black men filled seats in Southern state legislatures and U.S. Congress.

December 9, 1872-January 13, 1873
P.B.S. Pinchback serves as governor of Louisiana, becoming the first black to serve as state governor; however, resistance from white citizens sends him out of office after a month.

Freedom!

In December 1865, the Thirteenth Amendment was added to the United States Constitution. This amendment freed the slaves in every part of the country. However, freedom brought with it a lot of responsibility, and most freed slaves were not ready for the new reality of their lives.

After the Civil War, almost everyone in the South had to start over. This was hard enough for people who had lived on plantations all their lives, but it was much worse for freed slaves. Slaves definitely had excellent survival skills, but they had never had to worry about finding a place to live, growing or buying their own food, or finding a job.

The federal government quickly stepped in to help. In March 1865, Congress established the Bureau of Refugees, Freedmen, and Abandoned Lands. This agency's job was to assist

Many freed slaves worked for their former masters or other white farmers.

Freedmen's Village, Arlington, Virginia, 1865

freed slaves in adjusting to freedom. It soon became known as the Freedmen's Bureau.

The Freedmen's Bureau sent trainloads of food, clothing, and supplies to freed slaves and poor white refugees in the South. The bureau built hospitals and schools, as well as temporary quarters to house homeless refugees. The bureau also gave out more than 800,000 acres of abandoned or captured land to freed slaves and other refugees. Here, it was hoped, people could start their own farms. Unfortunately, most of the land meant for former slaves ended up in the hands of large plantation owners, railroads, and people who intended to sell the land at a huge profit. Many freed

February 1874
Blanche K. Bruce is elected to the U.S. Senate from Mississippi and becomes the first black senator to serve a complete six-year-term; Robert Smalls, a black hero of the Civil War, is elected to Congress as a representative of South Carolina.

March 1, 1875
Congress passes the Civil Rights Act, which provides blacks with equal rights in public places and transportation; however, the U.S. Supreme Court soon declares the Act against the law.

Blanche K. Bruce

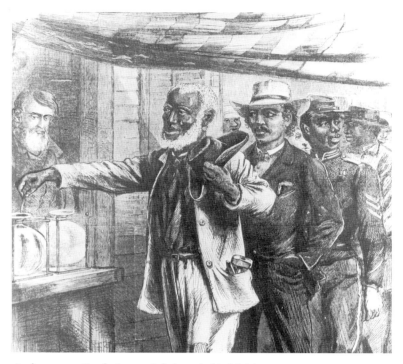

In the post-war South views varied about the blacks' right to vote.

Many white Southerners used violence and terror to keep blacks from receiving their rights. In December 1865, a group of six Confederate veterans formed a secret organization called the Ku Klux Klan. The KKK, as it came to be known, said its goal was to "protect the weak, the innocent, and the defenseless." In reality, the KKK's goal was to intimidate blacks and anyone who sympathized with them. KKK members wore robes and hoods to hide their identities. They often rode at night, burning homes, beating and murdering people, and spreading terror throughout the South. This climate of fear, combined with the "Black Codes" kept many black citizens from trying to vote at all. It would be almost one hundred years before the Civil Rights Movement and intervention by the federal government finally gave blacks the same rights and opportunities that white citizens enjoyed.

slaves were forced to work for their former masters or other white farmers. These workers became known as sharecroppers. These workers barely made enough money to survive and often had to pay for their own seeds and supplies. In addition, they had to turn part of their crop over to the landowners. Although they were free, sharecropper's living conditions were not much better than they had been during the days of slavery.

Efforts to give blacks the right to vote also ran into trouble. The Freedmen's Bureau tried to help, but sentiment against giving blacks the right to vote was too strong in the post-war South. Riots broke out in several cities, including New Orleans. Many Southern states passed laws called "Black Codes" that kept blacks from voting. Although the federal government passed the 14th and 15th Amendments to address these problems, it was many years before blacks truly had a voice in the government.

When it was all over, the Civil War had killed 620,000 soldiers, along with tens of thousands of civilians. Thousands more blacks were murdered during Reconstruction. The war had torn families apart and destroyed an entire way of life. However, the end of the Civil War brought a new beginning to the United States. The Civil War preserved the Union and killed slavery. The nation had survived its greatest threat and would soon develop into a major world power. And its citizens would finally be united as one nation.

The Ku Klux Klan wore robes and hoods.

March 1877
Rutherford B. Hayes inaugurated as president.

1879
The last federal troops leave South Carolina, ending the federal government's presence in the South.

South Carolina

Map of Major Battlefields and Civil War Sites

Minnesota

Wisconsin

Michigan

New Hampshire

Vermont

Maine

Iowa

New York

Massachusetts

Rhode Island

Connecticut

New York

Pennsylvania

Philadelphia

New Jersey

Gettysburg ★

Antietam ★

Ohio

Illinois

Indiana

Harpers Ferry ★

Washington D.C. Delaware

Manassas/Bull Run ★

Maryland

Brandy Station ★

West Virginia

Chancellorsville

Richmond

Kansas

Lexington ●

Virginia

Petersburg/ Five Forks

Missouri

Perryville ★

Appomattox ★

Kentucky

★ Wilson's Creek

Nashville

Tennessee

North Carolina

Raleigh ●

★ Pea Ridge

Franklin ★ ★ Murfreesboro

Doaksville ●

Chattanooga ★

South Carolina

Shiloh ★

Chickamauga ★

Columbia ●

Indian Territory

Arkansas

★ Atlanta

Augusta ●

Georgia

Charleston/ Ft. Sumter

Alabama

● Macon

Savannah ●

Mississippi

● Andersonville

★ Vicksburg

Montgomery ●

Louisiana

Texas

★ Port Hudson

Mobile ★

Baton Rouge ●

New Orleans ●

Florida

Union Territory

Confederate Territory

Border Slave States

Territories

● Cities

★ Battles

Glossary

Agriculture: Farming.

Ammunition: Bullets or artillery shells.

Amputate: To cut off.

Anesthetics: Drugs that put a person to sleep during surgery.

Arsenal: A place where guns and ammunition are stored.

Artillery: Large, powerful guns.

Assassination: To kill or murder someone who is well-known, especially a political figure.

Barracks: Buildings where soldiers live.

Blockade: To place warships around a port so that other ships cannot travel in or out of it.

Candidate: Someone who runs for office.

Casualty: A person who is injured or killed in battle.

Compromise: An agreement where both sides give up some of their demands.

Constitution: The written document containing the government principles and laws of the United States.

Convention: A meeting to choose candidates for an election.

Debates: Formal arguments where opposing sides offer their views on a topic and comment on their opponents' views.

Delegate: Someone who represents a government or group at a meeting.

Deserted: Ran away from the army.

Drill: To practice something over and over again.

Economy: The way a country runs its business and finances.

Emancipation: Freedom.

Industrial Revolution: A period of time where machines began to do work that was once done by hand, and also sped up and improved manufacturing.

Ironclad: Ships covered with iron plates for added protection from cannon fire.

Memoirs: A written account a person writes about his or her life.

Militias: Groups of citizens who are trained to fight but only serve during an emergency or a war.

Moral: A belief that something is right or wrong.

Pardoned: Forgiven.

Proclamation: An official announcement.

Regiments: Units of soldiers.

Secession: To formally withdraw from a country or organization.

Textile: Cloth.

Treason: The crime of betraying your country.

Tyrant: A leader who is cruel and unfair.

Picture Credits

Time line maps illustrated by Gabriel T. Byrne

p. 4 (top right): Library of Congress, LC-USZ62-89701

p. 4 (left & bottom right): © North Wind Picture Archives

p. 5 (top): © Bettmann/Corbis

p. 5 (bottom): © Hulton Archive/Getty Images

p. 6 (left): © North Wind Picture Archives

p. 6 (bottom): © Hulton Archive/Getty Images

p. 7 (top left): © North Wind Picture Archives

p. 7 (top right): Library of Congress, LC-USZ62-128709

p. 7 (bottom left): Library of Congress, LC-USZ62-11212

p. 7 (bottom right): © Hulton Archive/Getty Images

p. 8 (top): © North Wind Picture Archives

p. 8 (bottom left): © North Wind Picture Archives

p. 8 (bottom right): Library of Congress, LC-USZ62-128709

p. 9 (top): © Hulton Archives/Getty Images

p. 9 (right): © North Wind Picture Archives

p. 9 (bottom): © Hulton Archive/Getty Images

p. 10 (top): © North Wind Picture Archives

p. 10 (bottom left): Library of Congress, LC-USZ62-90724

p. 11 (top left): © North Wind Picture Archives

p. 11 (bottom left photo): © Fernando Bueno/Getty Images

p. 11 (bottom right): Library of Congress, LC-DIG-cwpbh-00879

p. 12 (top right): © Time Life Pictures/Getty Images

p. 12 (bottom right): © Hulton Archive/Getty Images

p. 13 (top left): Library of Congress, LC-USZ62-41678

p. 13 (center left): © Bettmann/Corbis

p. 13 (bottom left): Library of Congress, LC-USZC2-3775

p. 14 (left): © Hulton Archive/Getty Images

p. 14 (right): Library of Congress, LC-USZ62-119343

p. 15 (top): National Archives and Records Administration

p. 15 (center): © Hulton Archive/Getty Images

p. 15 (bottom right): © Hulton Archive/Getty Images

p. 16 (top): © Hulton Archive/Getty Images

p. 16 (bottom): © Hulton Archive/Getty Images

p. 17 (top left): Library of Congress, LC-USZC2-2706

p. 17 (top right): Library of Congress, LC-DIG-cwpbh-00882

p. 17 (bottom right): Library of Congress, LC-USZ62-99602

p. 18 (top & bottom): © Hulton Archive/Getty Images

p. 18 (center): Library of Congress, LC-USZ62-132563

p. 19 (top & center): © Hulton Archive/Getty Images

p. 19 (bottom): Private Collection, Peter Newark American Pictures/The Bridgeman Art Library International

p. 20 (top): © Getty Images

p. 20 (bottom): © Hulton Archive/Getty Images

p. 21 (top): Library of Congress, LC-DIG-cwpbh-00879

p. 21 (bottom): © Hulton Archive/Getty Images

p. 22 (left): Library of Congress, LC-DIG-cwpb-04352

p. 22 (right): © Hulton Archive/Getty Images

p. 22 (bottom): Private Collection, Peter Newark American Pictures/The Bridgeman Art Library International

p. 23 (top): Library of Congress, LC-USZ62-101468

p. 23 (center): Library of Congress, LC-DIG-cwpb-04402

p. 23 (bottom): Library of Congress, LC-USZC4-1768

p. 24 (top): © Hulton Archive/Getty Images

p. 24 (bottom right): Library of Congress, LC-DIG-cwpb-04402

p. 25 (top left): Library of Congress, LC-DIG-cwpb-03852

p. 25 (top right): Library of Congress, LC-USZC2-3775

p. 25 (center left): Library of Congress, LC-USZ62-91516

p. 25 (bottom left): © Getty Images

p. 25 (bottom right): Library of Congress, LC-USZ62-111519

p. 26 (top): © Hulton Archive/Getty Images

p. 26 (bottom): Library of Congress, LC-USZ62-10201

p. 27 (left & right): © Hulton Archive/Getty Images

p. 28 (left): Library of Congress, LC-USZ62-132209

p. 28 (right): Library of Congress, LC-USZ62-132204

p. 28 (bottom): Library of Congress, LC-DIG-cwpbh-04224

p. 29 (top): Black troops of the 54th Massachusetts Regiment during the assault of Fort Wagner, South Carolina, 18th July 1863. Private Collection, Peter Newark American Pictures/The Bridgeman Art Library International

p. 29 (bottom): Schlesinger Library, Radcliffe Institute, Harvard University/The Bridgeman Art Library International

p. 30 (top): © Corbis

p. 30 (bottom): © Hulton Archive/Getty Images

p. 31 (top left): © Corbis

p. 31 (center left): The twin Dahlgren guns of the Monitor's revolving turret. Private Collection, Peter Newark Military Pictures/The Bridgeman Art Library International

p. 31 (right): Private Collection, Peter Newark American Pictures/The Bridgeman Art Library International

p. 31 (bottom): Library of Congress, LC-USZ62-101468

p. 32 (left): Elizabeth Van Lew Papers, Manuscripts and Archives Division, The New York Public Library, Astor, Lenox and Tilden Foundations

p. 32 (right): Virginia Historical Society, Richmond, Virginia

p. 32 (bottom right): © Hulton Archive/Getty Images

p. 33 (top): Library of Congress, LC-DIG-cwpbh-03240

p. 33 (bottom left): © Hulton Archive/Getty Images

p. 33 (bottom right): Library of Congress, LC-USZ62-5616

p. 34: © Hulton Archive/Getty Images

p. 35 (top right): Library of Congress, LC-USZC4-1768

p. 35 (center right & bottom right): © Hulton Archive/Getty Images

p. 35 (bottom left): Library of Congress, LC-USZ62-103202

p. 36 (top left): Library of Congress, LC-DIG-pga-02502

p. 36 (bottom left): © Hulton Archive/Getty Images

p. 36 (bottom right): © Time Life Pictures/Getty Images

p. 37 (top): © Getty Images

p. 37 (bottom): Library of Congress, LC-USZ62-101486

p. 38: National Park Service Maps

p. 39 (top & bottom right): © Time Life Pictures/Getty Images

p. 39 (left): © Hulton Archive/Getty Images

p. 40: © Hulton Archive/Getty Images

p. 41 (top left & right): © Hulton Archive/Getty Images

p. 41 (bottom left): © Time Life Pictures/Getty Images

p. 42 (top right): Library of Congress, LC-DIG-cwpb-02226

p. 42 (center left): Library of Congress, LC-USZ62-101486

p. 42 (bottom right): © Getty Images

p. 43 (top): © Time Life Pictures/Getty Images

p. 43 (bottom): © Hulton Archive/Getty Images

p. 44 (top): © Hulton Archive/Getty Images

p. 44 (bottom left): Library of Congress, LC-USZ62-5616

p. 44 (bottom right): Library of Congress, LC-USZ62-25166

p. 45 (top & bottom): © Hulton Archive/Getty Images

p. 46 (top): © Bettmann/Corbis

p. 46 (bottom right): Library of Congress, LC-USZ62-121633

p. 47 (top): © Getty Images

p. 47 (bottom right): Library of Congress, LC-USZ62-89743

p. 48 (top): © Hulton Archive/Getty Images

p. 48: (bottom): Library of Congress, LC-USZ62-126311

p. 49 (top left): Library of Congress, LC-USZC4-5341

p. 49 (top right): Library of Congress, LC-USZ62-25166

p. 49 (center right): Library of Congress, LC-USZ62-5616

p. 49 (bottom left): Library of Congress, repro LC-DIG-cwpbh-03275

p. 49 (bottom right): © Hulton Archive/Getty Images

p. 50 (left): Library of Congress, LC-USZ62-77793

p. 50 (bottom right): Library of Congress, LC-USZ62-3983

p. 51 (left): Library of Congress, LC-DIG-cwpbh-00554

p. 51 (top right): Library of Congress, LC-USZ62-108004

p. 51 (bottom right): Library of Congress, LC-DIG-cwpbh-03863

p. 52 (top right): © Hulton Archive/Getty Images

p. 52 (left): © Time Life Pictures/Getty Images

p. 52 (bottom): Library of Congress, LC-DIG-cwpbh-05070

p. 53 (top left & right): © Hulton Archive/Getty Images

p. 53 (bottom left): Library of Congress, LC-USZ62-13091

p. 54: Map illustrated by Gabriel T. Byrne